Couture in the 21st Century

Couture in the 21st Century

By Deborah Bee
Portraits by Rankin

A&C BLACK

Harrods

First co-published by Harrods Publishing
and A&C Black Publishers Ltd, 2010

Harrods Publishing
87–135 Brompton Road
Knightsbridge
London
SW1X 7XL
Harrods.com

A&C Black Publishers Ltd
36 Soho Square
London
W1D 3QY
acblack.com

CIP catalogue records for this book are available
from the British Library and the US Library of
Congress

Every effort has been made to seek permission
to reproduce the images in this book.
Any omissions are unintentional. Please contact
Harrods Publishing for further details

Portraits: Rankin
Author: Deborah Bee
Design Director: Gerard Saint at Big Active
Design Assistant: Valerio Oliveri at Big Active
Publisher: Beth Hodder
Picture Editor: Dalia Nassimi
Editorial Assistant: Laura Jordan
Copy-Editors: Lisa Hillman, Tim Cumming,
Nicolette Thompson
Production Manager: Hayley Ellis

Harrods
Managing Director: Michael Ward
Image Director: Mark Briggs
Fashion Director: Marigay McKee
Advertising Sales Director: Guy Cheston
Head of PR: Amber Pepper

A&C Black Publishers
Visual Arts Publisher: Susan James
Sales and Marketing Director: David Wightman
Fashion Publicity: Ellen Williams

Special thanks to Felicity Green, Mark Eastment
and Amy de la Haye at the V&A, Omer Acar, the
lovely team at Harrods Publishing, Kirsty Allen,
Camilla Hall, Rachell Smith, Dominic Storer,
Andrew Davies, Neil Dawson, Michael Tinney,
Gabriel Lloret and Max Montgomery

Portraits shot on location at: Ritz Paris; Hotel
Principe di Savoia, Milan; The Lowell, New York
Book Design by Big Active
Typeset using Lexia by Dalton Magg
Reproduction by Zebra
Printing by Push

Cover Graphics: Siggi Eggertsson at Big Active
Page 2: 'Bar' suit by Christian Dior from the Corolle
Collection 1947, later dubbed the New Look
Page 6: Velvet gown by Balenciaga, 1952

Contents

Foreword
Deborah Bee

IF EVER A TERM HAS BEEN misappropriated, "haute couture" is it. The phrase is tossed around casually on the high street, and newspapers are only too happy to apply the term where it is, quite hilariously, not applicable – at worst, even to a new supermarket clothing range. What is perhaps more surprising is that even fashion designers struggle to agree on what haute couture means today.

Strictly defined as "high sewing", haute couture has evolved from the days when it was invented by the Chambre Syndicale de la Confection et de la Couture pour Dames et Fillettes in 1868. Back then, haute couture was the equivalent of men's tailoring – the creation of exclusive, handmade garments, after a series of fittings, to the highest possible standard. To belong to the Chambre Syndicale, the couture house had to adhere to a rigid set of rules, such as employing a certain number of people in its workshops and presenting at least 50 original designs twice a year during the official couture schedule. Similar rules still exist and, although the number of couture houses has dropped significantly – from 106 in 1946 to nine for Autumn/Winter 2010 – 2010 saw a surprising rise in the number of orders.

The general decline in the size of the industry, however, is not at all reflected in the interest in the skills that couture represents. For the past 250 years, haute couture has been underpinned by a range of specialist crafts that remains unequalled in any other industry. From embroidery to buttons, millinery to gloves, lace to handmade flowers, complicated construction to bows, the French ateliers have been perfecting their arts for generations, with a strict hierarchy that ensures the highest level of workmanship. And it is these skills that inspire today's most successful designers.

For despite the dwindling number of couture houses, the intricately crafted details inherent in haute couture are now in demand for ready-to-wear. Over the past decade, a desire for this superlative quality and embellishment has led to a renewed interest in the kinds of finishes that were once the preserve of a rarefied world – and that interest is helping to make couture relevant for a new generation. Many fashion houses are including special pieces in each collection – pieces that are one of a kind and represent many hours' work.

While designers agree about the inspirations of the past, they are divided in their definitions of haute couture: one side argues that it is discreetly elegant, made-to-measure garments for the exceptional few; the other side believes it is a gorgeous spectacle that simply acts as a platform from which to sell something else, such as accessories or perfume. And somewhere in between, couture represents a new way of thinking about fashion, where provenance and quality are more important than label lust. It is exhilarating and inspirational – and the very pinnacle of fashion fantasy.

Couture in the 21st Century celebrates the greatest couturiers of all time through the eyes, and contemporary designs, of the world's finest fashion designers. With interviews, portraits and examples of historic inspirations, the book demonstrates the influence of the past on shaping the future.

"We have Charles Worth to thank for starting it all" – John Galliano 2010 [1]

History of Couture

CONTENDERS FOR THE TITLE of "King of Couture" are a matter of some debate. Those chosen by our 21st-century designers are all worthy, and our interviewees are nothing if not dogmatic. But in terms of history and far-reaching influence, our designers universally agree with John Galliano, that we really do have Charles Worth to thank for starting it all.

Back in the mid-19th century, Charles Worth was something of an anomaly. Since 1675, dressmaking had become a largely female trade. Yet Worth had become the toast of fashionable society, and his extravagant creations underpinned it, with the wealthiest ladies attending every grand occasion of state or masquerade ball decked out in his silk and satin confections. But Worth's reputation for creating the most awe-inspiring designs was tinged with an undercurrent of scandal.

During the early days of his Parisian couture house, the social mores of the times deemed it highly inappropriate for a man to be allowed such close proximity to his clients. And later, when Worth had fully developed his rather dictatorial style, many newspapers published literary stabs at the King of Couture's diktats. One French cartoon called Worth's crinolines "...difficult to manage, impossible on the omnibus, liable to conflagration, and turning madame into a triangle".[2] And in the late 1860s, Charles Dickens described him as a perfect gentleman, but also noted that "he officiates with all the gravity of a diplomatist who holds the fate of the world locked up in the drawers of his brain".[3]

But for all his embroidered trains and lace-frilled bustles, Worth's reputation today is not built on his design inspiration. Although he was and is revered for his extraordinary cutting, innovative, magnificent designs and elaborate fabrics, it is his organisational skills for which he is most remembered. For Charles Worth established haute couture. He was the first designer to properly dictate fashion, and because of his success, he was forced to set up an industry around him. It is thanks to Worth setting up in France that haute couture and Paris are inextricably linked.

As a young man, Worth had worked in two mercer's shops, the first in London and the second in Paris, in 1846. Maison Gagelin specialised in

Above: The first King of Couture, Charles Worth, whose styles dominated European aristocratic society in the mid-19th century
Left: Putting on the finishing touches at the atelier of the great Parisian designer Worth, in Paris, 1907

the very finest hand-loomed silks from Lyon, and Worth's job was to sell mantles and shawls – the only ready-made garments suitable for a lady of refinement. The custom of the time dictated that, on desiring a new outfit, a lady should first visit the mercer to choose her fabric, then take the fabric to her favourite dressmaker to realise a design that would have been arrived at through some detailed consultation.

Worth saw an opportunity to provide a swifter and simpler approach. After a certain amount of opposition from his employers, Worth was allowed to open a dress department in the store, making up some very simple summer styles from the elaborate in-house fabrics. Despite a degree of disapproval, the idea took off, and highly respectable women began visiting the salon for Worth's dresses.

In 1858, Worth set up his own couture house, and, once installed in 7 rue de la Paix, his rich evening gowns won the patronage of Empress Eugénie; this in turn opened the doors to European royalty and international society. But as the cultivated elite competed with each other in Worth's fancy creations, a demand was generated for better structure and coordination for the fashion house. Hence Worth established the first formal seasonal collections, presented on living, breathing models instead of mannequins.

A system of haute couture evolved that stuck to certain rigid rules, set in place by the Chambre Syndicale de la Haute Couture Parisienne, founded in Paris in 1868. It became routine for the head of a fashion house to select sketches from a bank of freelance designers. Different designers worked for different houses, sometimes designing for more than one house at the same time. Once the sketches had been selected, a toile (a calico replica) would be created, with specialised workers taking on the sleeves, bodices or skirts.

When all the component parts had been completed, the finished toile would be constructed and, if this met with approval, the garment would be made up in a specially selected fabric. At a couture house's seasonal presentation – Spring/Summer in January and Autumn/Winter in July – at least 50 outfits were shown to an audience made up of customers and authorised buyers. The designs were then made up for the clients or sold as patterns, either in linen or paper.

Clients would attend a series of fittings that could take weeks to complete, during which any fit or style alterations would be incorporated. For example, long sleeves rather than short may be required, or empire line rather than a fitted waist, and it was up to the couturier and his senior staff to ensure that these alterations corresponded with the overarching aesthetic of the house.

Once a silhouette had become popular in a

Left: Madame Jeanne Lanvin, famous for her "robes de style", based on 18th-century designs, in her private office, 1946
Below: Madeleine Vionnet, whose mastery of the bias cut has ensured she remains a legend for today's couturiers
Below right: Paul Poiret with his models, photographed on the platform at Victoria Railway Station, London, 1924

fashion house, it may have remained there for several seasons, made up into different fabrics according to the trends. The signature of each house was determined by the personal taste of the head, who would issue instructions concerning the final trims. Embroidery, lace, fabric flowers, beads, braid, and ribbons would all have been employed to give the garment an original, hand-crafted finish.

When Charles Worth died in 1895, his house was continued by four generations of Worths. Although his very good taste, masterly attitude and innovative designs are celebrated, the haute couture system is his lasting legacy.

High fashion at the beginning of the 20th century remained extravagant and luxurious. But as their role in society began to change, women increasingly occupied public spaces, and a demand grew for more practical clothing. Madame Paquin became popular for her day suits created for the more active woman. In her coterie of designers she counted Léon Bakst – a set designer whose creations for the Ballets Russes were influencing new trends – and Paul Iribe, an illustrator who later went on to work with the radical couturier Paul Poiret. Although Paquin had retired by 1920, women's attitudes towards the corseted silhouette had significantly altered during her heyday.

Meanwhile, Jacques Doucet, an extravagant designer, had won the hearts of high society in the late 19th century with designs inspired by historical paintings. He restructured his lace, silk mousseline and satin gowns in a bid to rid women of their corsets – a popular move among young, progressive ladies.

And in an industry now dominated almost entirely by men, Lucille was pioneering the concept of globalisation by simultaneously operating her couture houses in London, New York and Paris. Her fashion legacies, however, are her soft pastel colour schemes, her seductive lingerie and being behind the first proper fashion parades, albeit in a garden!

In the early part of the 20th century, the man, according to Christian Dior, "who came along and changed it all" was Paul Poiret. The son of a cloth merchant who joined Doucet in 1899, Poiret was taken on by the House of Worth in 1901. According to Poiret's autobiography, Gaston Worth recognised a need for change, and explained to Poiret that although they still possessed the richest clientele, "sometimes Princesses take the omnibus". Poiret was asked to create a line of practical dresses to suit more practical lifestyles. "We are like some restaurant," Gaston continued, "which would refuse to serve aught but truffles. It is therefore necessary for us to create a department of fried potatoes."[4]

Poiret launched his own couture house in 1903. His Bohemian style, almost barbaric sense of colour and loose silhouette were considered too bizarre and too avant-garde to be worn by most women at that time, even though his influence is now considered far-reaching. In 1908 Poiret employed Iribe's considerable illustration abilities to create a series of limited-edition, hand-printed albums of his designs called *Les Robes de Paul Poiret*. The illustrations demonstrated Poiret's technique for using the garment to display Art Deco motifs. But Poiret's heart was in silhouette. As Dior said, "He used to take the material in his hands, drape it softly round the figure of his mannequin, without worrying too much about how it fell, to produce an astonishing colour effect: then a snip here and there with the scissors, a few pins, and the dress was ready!"[5]

The hierarchy of La Grande Couture was already well established during Poiret's reign as King of Couture. There were buyers who purchased fabrics, embroideries and buttons and estimated the cost of each final piece. The cutters and tailors (usually men), and sewing technicians and dressmakers (usually women), worked under the premières – the couturiers' right-hand women – who oversaw that the sketches translated into completed garments. The premières stood in for the couturier when dealing with customers, and were respected by clients for their aesthetic opinions. And there were saleswomen who dealt directly with the customers, making any changes to the garment that the client required.

Poiret said of these changes: "A Parisienne never adopts a model without making in it changes of capital importance, and particularising it to suit herself. An American woman chooses the model presented to her, and buys it just as it is, while a Parisienne wants it to be blue if it is green, or garnet if it is blue, and adds a fur collar and changes the sleeves, and suppresses the bottom buttons. The high art of dressmaking consists precisely in developing the individuality of each woman."[6]

The most shocking pre-World War I fashion statement came from Coco Chanel, with her *sportif* trend. Having established couture salons in Paris and the seaside resorts of Deauville and Biarritz, she created lightweight clothes with no linings, employed soft jersey for cardigans and sweaters and, in 1920, created a craze for wide-legged trousers and matelot tops. After World War I, she was a walking advertisement for confident, independent women who wanted to be in fashion without being a slave to it. Her tweed collarless jacket and matching skirt, originally the preserve of progressive women, eventually became a classic. Chanel's impact on couture cannot be underestimated. At the height of her fame in the 1930s, she employed over 4,000 workers.[7] She was the first couturier to spot the potential revenue in fragrance and, while Poiret had developed a scent before she did, Chanel gave her version her own name. The sales of fragrance have underpinned the couture industry ever since.

Amidst the horror of World War I, fashion necessarily became more utilitarian, and the most successful designers were working in a less flamboyant style. But their careers were interrupted by the austerity of the time, including that of Frenchman Jean Patou. Launching his house in 1914, Patou reopened in 1919 in Paris and was successful immediately. The trend was for a simpler, more natural style for women who were active, and Patou continued the theme. He dominated the couture scene in the '20s and mid-'30s with sports-inspired clothing that included calf-length skirts and sleeveless cardigans.

Elsewhere, Jeanne Lanvin had developed a highly original aesthetic that contrasted sharply with the mood of the times. Best known for her "robes de style", she became popular just before World War I. Her signature style consisted of fitted bodices with long, flowing skirts and hooped hems that were based on 18th-century designs. Lanvin's first foray into fashion, however, was a millinery shop in Paris in 1889. During the early years of the 20th century, she made dresses for her daughter that caught the attention of her customers. She moved into dressmaking and became well known for making matching garments for mothers and daughters.

Lanvin is perhaps best loved for her use of embroidery inspired by Orientalism, and for the shade of cornflower blue that so often appeared in her collections and that later became known as Lanvin blue.

As Lanvin was trimming her pleated dresses with divinely pretty embroidery, Madeleine Vionnet was busy mastering the art of the bias cut. Vionnet had learned the ropes at Doucet in 1907. Despite opening her own house in 1912, it wasn't until after World War I that she became known as one of the most innovative and important couturiers of her day.

Vionnet dispensed with corsets altogether and instead allowed the body to create its own curves. Her speciality was in draping on the stand, using fabric that had been cut on the cross and then hung for sometimes many months in order for it to find its natural drop. Famous for working on miniature models, Vionnet also mastered diagonal seaming and faggoting in order to construct her bias-cut creations. Although her dresses looked nothing on the hanger, once on the body the smooth, elegant shape formed by her favourite fabrics –

typically silk crepe, crepe de Chine, satin and gabardine – was unparalleled. Her technical contribution to the world of couture is never underestimated.

Elsa Schiaparelli – an Italian-born, American-educated designer who moved to Paris in 1922 – drew attention to her artistic skills with a trompe l'oeil bow sweater. In 1927 she had enough fans to open a couture salon, and launched her distinctive aesthetic on the world with amusing, sometimes shocking, always striking designs. Sharing ideas with her friends Salvador Dalí and Jean Cocteau, she created a hat in the shape of a shoe, a dress decorated with a painting of a lobster by Dalí, and another dress in the shape of a skeleton; she also developed a fabric decorated in newsprint.

Although the history books depict Schiaparelli as an avant-garde rebel, most of what she sold was fairly restrained. While her wealthy international clients were undoubtedly charmed by her clever integration of art and design, her evening gowns and tailored suits were highly sophisticated and elegant. She also championed innovation, introducing tweed for eveningwear, eschewing buttons in favour of zips, and adopting the use of shoulder pads in the late '30s, after Hollywood costume designer Adrian had all but invented the idea for Joan Crawford.

Also popular at this time was Robert Piguet, who opened his couture house in 1933 and specialised in dramatic gowns and tailored suits. His sophisticated aesthetic attracted a coterie of young design talent that turned out to be the next generation of great designers, including Pierre Balmain, Marc Bohan, Christian Dior and Hubert de Givenchy.

Lucien Lelong's first collection appeared in 1914 and, with a background in textiles, he was especially noted for his opulent fabrics. But as head of the Chambre Syndicale during World War II, he made it possible for 92 couture houses to remain open during the Occupation, rather than move to Berlin and Vienna as Hitler had intended, having recognised the cultural cachet of the couture industry.[8] During the Occupation between 1940 and 1944, however, Paris was effectively cut off from the rest of the world. With London and New York forced to rely on their own homegrown talent, the Parisian couture houses had to either downsize dramatically or close altogether.

In 1937 Jacques Fath and Jean Desses had both opened couture houses in Paris. The former became famous for his hourglass designs once the war ended and developed a keen following in the States. Desses returned to Egypt and Greece after the war and then became famous for his draped designs, whose roots were in his

JEAN PATOU

heritage. Also deriving inspiration from classical culture, Alix Barton – later known as Madame Grès – made toiles for major Parisian fashion houses in the late '20s and early '30s. She opened her own house in 1934, closed down for part of the Occupation, and reopened in 1942. Grès' signature pleating was an intense labour of love that only a trained eye can even begin to appreciate. Light as air on the outside, massively complicated on the inside, her evening gowns took weeks to create. It is widely believed that there has yet to be a designer who can replicate her skill.

While the practicalities of life in the '30s dictated less restrictive clothing, 1936 saw a resurgence of neo-romanticism in Parisian couture, with designers reintroducing crinolines and bustles, especially for eveningwear. British-born Charles James was one of the earliest exponents of this romantic revival, and during the war he took up a position at Elizabeth Arden in New York. James' spiral-skirted ball gowns were perhaps his signature design, and turned him into a star in America. At the same time, another king of cutting – Cristóbal Balenciaga – was honing his craft back in the couture capital, Paris.

Born in the Basque region of Spain, Balenciaga trained to be a tailor from the age of 12 and could create fairly complicated designs by the time he was 14. His opened his first fashion house in San Sebastián in Spain but, following the onset of the Spanish Civil War, he was forced to leave his homeland. Through loans from friends, he was able to open a couture house in Paris in 1937 at 10 Avenue George V.

During the war years his reputation grew, with his reopened Spanish houses attracting international clients. The Spanish newspapers reported that "women from all over the world cross frontiers to buy his creations".[9] In 1931 Poiret had predicted that fashion needed a new hero who would "set women free as I did in my day".[10] Balenciaga is regarded as being this hero for, unlike many of his contemporaries, he understood the entire fashion process, from the design to the cutting and sewing. Having understood the rules, he was able to subvert them and create hugely fashion-forward designs of restrained, pared-down simplicity, with no agenda for following trends.

Even when Christian Dior launched, Carmel Snow of *Harper's Bazaar* praised Balenciaga's seeming simplicity and unmatched mastery of execution.[11] Many of the world's top designers believe that this mastery remains unsurpassed, even today, and he is always held as being the couturiers' couturier.

However, in 1947 the fashion world was presented with a revolution. Dior's debut Corolle

Above left: Elsa Schiaparelli studies the charts of her new collection, in 1938
Left: Jean Patou ca 1929
Above: Coco Chanel, in front of her favourite Coromandel screens, 1937
Above right: Alix Barton, later known as Madame Grès, 1933
Right: Cristóbal Balenciaga in Paris, 1927

collection, quickly dubbed the New Look, was the starting point of a golden age of couture, when Paris rediscovered its authority on the international fashion scene. Dior reinstated in fashion what he called "*joie de vivre*", with a romantic hourglass silhouette.[12] Tiny, corseted waists were accentuated with full, layered skirts and padding over the hips, while jackets and gowns were cut to draw attention to the décolleté. The style was hailed as fresh and original by the press and became a roaring success for the new house.

Yet Dior's New Look was not met with universal approval. Against a backdrop of post-war austerity, Dior had replaced practical tweed tailoring made using a conservative amount of fabric with vast-skirted dresses and suits. His critics, many of them among the general public, felt Dior was imposing an impossible dream. On the one hand it was unequivocal that Dior had reinstated Paris as the epicentre of the fashion world. On the other hand, he caused a political outrage that made international headlines.

It was not long before the international fashion scene had adopted the New Look, and for the next 10 years Dior raised and lowered hems at whim, becoming known as a "dictator of fashion" for his trends that required women to reinvent their wardrobes each season.[13]

As Dior embarked upon tours in America, Hardy Amies was specialising in tweed tailored suits in London and day dresses for the then-Princess Elizabeth, and Norman Hartnell was working towards the future queen's coronation dress.

Back in Paris, Hubert de Givenchy opened up a couture house in 1952. Years at Jacques Fath and later at Schiaparelli had helped him develop a highly individual style with a purity of line not dissimilar to Balenciaga's. Givenchy first became famous for a blouse. Said to have been so lacking in funds that he was forced to used cotton, Givenchy designed a blouse made of shirting with a wide-open neck, narrow waist and fully frilled sleeves of *broderie anglaise*. Named after the model Bettina Graziani, the style put Givenchy on the fashion map.

However, his costumes for Audrey Hepburn in *Sabrina* (1954) and his continuing relationship with Hepburn turned her into a style icon and Givenchy into a household name who determined many of the key trends in the '50s.

Ten years after his seminal New Look, Christian Dior died suddenly of a heart attack. As Paris mourned, it fell upon Marcel Boussac, Dior's financial backer, to appoint a successor. Having decided to close the house, Boussac was persuaded to take a punt on a rather fragile young man who had started at Dior just two years earlier as Dior's junior assistant.

Top: Christian Dior at a fitting in London, in the '50s
Above: Hubert de Givenchy with his muse, Audrey Hepburn, in the '50s
Above right: Christian Lacroix at the launch of his Spring/Summer 1988 collection
Below right: Hardy Amies, the dressmaker appointed to Queen Elizabeth II, in 1950

Yves Mathieu-Saint-Laurent launched his first collection in 1958 and – with a modern, looser silhouette that owed all of its heritage to Dior – was said to have "saved France" with his new Trapeze collection.[14]

The triangular shapes were soon followed by the Arc line of autumn '58, the Long line of '59 and a shortened version of the hobble skirt for his fourth collection, which did not sit particularly comfortably with Dior traditionalists. However, the furore caused by the lean silhouette was nothing in comparison to the '60s Beat collection. In tune with the radical youth of the times, Saint Laurent had updated the street looks being adopted by art students. Leather jackets, bubble skirts and skinny turtlenecks were translated into luxury fabrics like cashmere and crocodile in an attempt to suit the sophisticated arena of couture. However, his forward thinking was way ahead of both his house and his customers. Boussac despised the collection, and even Saint Laurent himself, years later, admitted that the street inspirations must have felt "very inelegant to a lot of people sitting on the gilt chairs of a couture salon".[15] With hindsight, this collection was one of the most important in fashion history, the first time that subcultural styles had influenced the catwalk. At the time, the collection was panned and, with unfortunate timing, it was at this point that Saint Laurent was called up to serve in the French army as a conscript in the Algerian War. When he returned some months later, having been discharged through illness, his former colleague Bohan had been appointed as head designer at Dior, leaving Saint Laurent with nothing else to do but begin his own fashion house.

As Saint Laurent recuperated, and sued Dior for breach of contract, his partner, Pierre Bergé, got to grips with setting up a couture house. With the money from the lawsuit, as well as further backing, Saint Laurent took over the premises of a hotel in the 16th arrondissement and launched the first collection on 29th January 1962.

For the next half decade, the house became known for sophisticated reworks of traditional garments with pea jackets and workmen's smocks, knickerbockers and trouser suits appearing in fine wool and silk satin. But perhaps his most famous pieces – those that will belong to him forever – are the Mondrian dress of 1965 and the Le Smoking tuxedo suits of 1966. That same year, Saint Laurent launched his ready-to-wear label, Rive Gauche, and shortly afterwards chose to return to a much more glamorous aesthetic for his couture line, which became his lifelong signature.

Meanwhile, a new generation of rebellious teenagers was moving fashion in a new direction. Following Saint Laurent's lead, other designers began to accept the reversal of the trickle-down effect, appropriating street styles for couture. Bohan cultivated a pop spirit at Dior while his previous cohort, Pierre Cardin, supplied The Beatles with their collarless jackets in 1963 and introduced futuristic Space-Age designs in such technically advanced fabrics as PVC. Goggles, mid-calf boots, trapeze minicoats and cutout dresses were also advocated by André Courrèges.

Valentino Garavani put Parisians on high alert when he began designing his most elegant concoctions from Rome in 1962. As the energetic '60s slipped into a more languid, casual mood, the likes of Valentino and Saint Laurent owned the couture runways.

But what is generally perceived to be a flat time in the history of couture was given a shot in the arm by the arrival of Christian Lacroix and Karl Lagerfeld. Although Lagerfeld had been a contemporary of Saint Laurent, a short sojourn into art history meant that he left the industry until 1967, when he became a consultant for Fendi. His most famous tenure has been at Chanel, which he began in 1983 and where he reigns supreme to this day.

Another trailblazer, Lacroix got to grips with couture at Patou from 1981 until he opened his own salon in 1987. A distinctively eclectic approach to design saw a mishmash of patterns and textures appear in thoroughly off-kilter yet elaborate costumes. His lack of convention and sheer chutzpah won him a raft of fans and a following that remains loyal to this day.

The king of '80s couture is widely accepted to be Gianni Versace, whose star-studded shows were as spectacular as his vibrant gowns. At the other end of the celebrity-courting scale, Azzedine Alaïa, though not strictly a couturier, was quietly winning hearts and minds with his technical inventiveness. While Jean Paul Gaultier was reinventing corsetry as outerwear and Oscar de la Renta was setting in stone his Belle Époque approach, John Galliano was studying costume at the V&A as part of his course at Central Saint Martins. His graduation show was a precursor for a long line of fashion spectaculars, with a riot of 18th-century French revolution-inspired designs. His move to Dior in 1996, together with Alexander McQueen's arrival at Givenchy, marked a regeneration of haute couture. Both designers carried something of the past with them: a taste for romance and reinvention; poetic inspiration and wit; and a reliance on the sort of traditional craftsmanship that only a couture house can deliver. As Galliano said in 2010, "The entire process of couture is magical – from research to the making of the toile, fittings to the final show – it is the craftsmanship, the skill, the hours and the creativity that go into each and every detail. It is pure magic."[16] Long may it continue.

Couture in the 21st Century

Giorgio Armani

FOR ME, THE VERY BEST IDEAS come from the ability to respond creatively to the infinite opportunities that life offers. In 1975, almost by chance, I reinvented the jacket by rethinking the construction and removing the lining. The idea of transposing the jacket into the world of couture was a challenge I could not ignore. It was an opportunity to bring something that I consider to be absolutely indispensable to the point of absolute perfection.

But the raison d'être for me creating a couture collection was to allow me to express the most sumptuous facet of fashion, as well as letting me develop a broader appreciation of my work among those who already share a common interest in the Armani aesthetic.

It always felt like a natural progression for me to create my haute couture line, Armani Privé, but at the same time it was a carefully considered move. It was a challenge that I set myself and that I confronted with considerable excitement. And it gave me immense pleasure, as does every new venture. But this was a particularly special case, because designing my own couture collection was always a dream – and now it has come true.

But even before I started the very first collection I was very aware that I had to concentrate on expressing a modern outlook. It would have been all too easy to fall into the trap of creating something that was very dated or caught in a particular period, however magnificent that might have looked.

This is a risk inherent in the haute couture scene. There are so many rituals associated with couture that are appropriate to a society so firmly rooted in the past. But I wanted to focus on a vision of the future. I wanted a contemporary feel that would suit the woman of the 21st century.

I would say that Coco Chanel laid the foundations of modern fashion. What interests me is that she knew how to create a spontaneous version of couture. It was easy to wear, with a quality of simplicity that, to a certain extent, anticipated the world of prêt-à-porter that was about to come.

In other words, it was not statuesque. There was nothing excessive about it, no exaggerated flounces. Instead it was something made with precision and subtlety, with a timeless grace. If it were not for her, I think that fashion would be very different today. And while Chanel was reinventing womenswear, I would say that Cristóbal Balenciaga was exerting a powerful influence on fashion. He had a masterly grasp of the architectural quality of fashion that has perhaps never been fully appreciated.

And if I could have worked with one of them, I guess it would be Chanel. After her, I would say that Vionnet would have been interesting

"Couture's purpose is to make us dream – that goes for the designer as well as the woman who is wearing it. But the dream needs to be anchored in reality"

to work with as she was introducing the bias cut; Madame Grès when she was creating her peplums; or Marcel Rochas when he was designing his lace corset. To have been close to any of these extraordinary giants when they were working on their iconic pieces would have been a magnificent experience.

Luxury today is regaining its authentic value, based on a new appreciation of the perfect, the exceptional and the very rare. This contemporary version of luxury has its roots firmly secured in tradition. This higher demand for the most luxurious goods is a reaction against the current economic crisis, as it also signifies a reduction in demand at every other level, forcing brands to focus on the ever-important quality of integrity.

For a brand to succeed in this climate, it is important that the value of goods is reflected in the price; that is not to say that the price has to be low – not by any means. It means that the price has to be appropriate.

Everything about couture is magic. Everything depends upon manual skills, craftsmanship and infinite patience. I could spend hours marvelling at the dexterity of the petites mains, as the French call their dressmakers. Without their work, haute couture as it stands would simply not exist.

Today, couture is the culmination of the meticulous and the fantastic. It is the ultimate expression of something unique and rare that transcends the laws of commerce to provide a fresh, modern demonstration of craftsmanship.

Couture is fashion in its purest form, an extraordinary phenomenon that, though controlled by tradition, can also be very futuristic. Couture's purpose is to make us dream – that goes for the designer as well as the woman who is wearing it. But the dream needs to be anchored in reality. After all, what would be the point of an unwearable dress? It would be a contradiction of terms. Haute couture is magic – that is certainly true. But it is also a dress.

There are plenty of fashion designers today who have thrown themselves into the world of high fashion and who have convinced themselves – and those people around them – that calling something "tailor made" is enough to justify its status as haute couture. It is not. Haute couture is something very special and incredibly complex. It is explicitly intended for certain highly influential customers who love exclusive luxury. Valentino understood this. So does Karl. Both have contributed significantly to preserving the allure of couture.

It takes a special kind of designer to fulfil the requirements of a couturier. You need to have a comprehensive technical knowledge of fabrics as well as an understanding of anatomy. Then it is

possible to produce a dress that is an architectural dream. But also important – equally important, in fact – is the ability to build and maintain interpersonal relationships with customers. Trust is absolutely vital in this circle.

"Haute couture is something very special and incredibly complex. It is explicitly intended for certain highly influential customers who love exclusive luxury"

Biographical Notes

Giorgio Armani was born on 11th July 1934, and studied medicine and photography before completing military service in Italy. His first job in fashion was as a merchandiser for the Milan department store La Rinascente. He joined Nino Cerruti as a designer in 1961 and stayed with Cerruti until 1970. He launched his eponymous fashion house in 1975 with men's and women's ready-to-wear collections.

Armani's unstructured jackets are considered to have revolutionised fashion and tailoring in the 80s; in 1982, Armani became the first fashion designer since Christian Dior in 1957 to appear on the cover of *Time* magazine. Since the '90s, the Armani name has been synonymous with red-carpet glamour, and his designs have graced some of the world's most influential stars, from Julia Roberts, Angelina Jolie and George Clooney to Lady Gaga's tour outfits; the Beckhams fronted an Armani underwear campaign.

In response to demand, Armani debuted his haute couture collection, Armani Privé, in 2005. To date, Giorgio Armani S.p.A employs over 5,000 people and consists of many labels, including Armani Collezioni, Emporio Armani, Armani Exchange, Armani Junior and Armani/Casa.

Giorgio Armani has been feted with numerous honours, including Italy's highest government awards: Commendatore dell'Ordine al Merito della Repubblica, and Grande Ufficiale dell'Ordine al Merito della Repubblica. He also received the award for Best International Designer, Lifetime Achievement Award for menswear and for art and fashion from the Council of Fashion Designers of America. In 2000, the Guggenheim Museum in New York celebrated Armani's work with a career retrospective, which then toured the world.

Opposite: From Giorgio Armani's Autumn/Winter 2010 Armani Privé couture collection shown in Paris in July 2010. The collection was a subtle nod to the ladylike elegance of the '50s and old Hollywood in a palette of ambers, from caramel to coral. Daywear was represented by ruched crepe silk sheath dresses and softly pleated knee length skirts paired with clutch bags and waist-skimming peplum jackets, including one in crocodile skin. The red carpet-ready eveningwear included gold and bronze gowns heavily embellished with beads and sequins, and floor-length caramel-coloured gowns with folds of silk satin

Above: A Pierre Mourgue illustration of a Marcel Rochas dress from 1949. Mourgue worked regularly for Vogue in the '20s and '30s, when Rochas' couture and Madame Rochas perfume were taking Paris by storm

Right: A floor-length red velvet evening dress for mid-season wear by Chanel, from February 1935. For Armani, Chanel "laid the foundations of fashion" and anticipated the rise of prêt-à-porter

Antonio Berardi

SOMETIMES I LOOK AT MODERN ART and I don't really get it. I think, well, I could've done that. And if I could've done it, I don't want it. So when I consider couture I think, well, I can't do amazing featherwork; I'm not an amazing embroiderer; I'm not the most amazing person to make a corset – but when all the people who can do those things collaborate on one thing, then it becomes special. That is a work of art. That is couture.

I've never worked in a couture atelier. It is still one of my dreams to be privy to such a wondrous workshop. But I did once work with 14 bobbin lacemakers to make a dress for one of my shows. Like a Vionnet dress, there were no seams, as everything was worked out prior to the making, and the bobbins were hand-carved from bone. It took nearly four months as it was passed from hand to hand, but the result was incredible. It also took around 45 minutes to lace Naomi Campbell into it.

Couture originally came about because of a very specific need by women. Men had their tailors. Women wanted something that could be made especially for them, something perfect and sublime. Madeleine Vionnet was one of the first great couturiers back in the '20s and '30s. Her attention to the female form made her a formidable force. Even by today's standards, she is a genius.

There is one particular dress that she made out of octagons or hexagons of fabric that decrease in size, and they form the body shape, so it is a decorative piece, but at the same time there are no seams. She imposed form through the illusion of embellishment, carefully concealing minuscule adjustments in the process. At times Vionnet's work is akin to a modern architect's streamlined vocabulary of ornament, to serve the compositional needs.

All couture is a bit like architecture; it relies upon the synergy between the client and the designer. It has to satisfy the surroundings as well as the existing physical properties.

To a degree, I am on the side of Christian Lacroix when he said that "haute couture should be fun, foolish and almost unwearable", but I also love that it should be the Rolls-Royce of fashion – the ultimate, the most sublime, born of fantasy and passion but wearable. Couture sits at the top of the fashion trinity, crowning both prêt-à-porter and licensing, but it needs to be worn, to be seen to be believed, to be appreciated and, essentially, to envelop the wearer and make her feel like she is the only person that exists.

We are living in a time when people expect so much from fashion. Even in the space of five years, fashion has evolved so much. Perhaps we

"Some designers are a bit afraid of couture... afraid to show fantasy because they feel the public is thinking this is not utilitarian, it isn't wearable enough"

are all trying a little bit too hard because there are so many of us now. There are so many brands. And you think to yourself, I have to do something amazing, every time. But we are losing the fundamentals of what clothes are about. What I try to do is very much what Phoebe Philo is doing at Céline – beautifully made clothes – because we all appear to have forgotten the importance of craftsmanship.

I look around at brands that are bigger than mine, and I wonder how they can get away with charging so much. It is so wrong when you know how much things have cost them. I know where designers are getting their clothes made – I know how much their fabrics cost – and even taking into consideration the various shops' mark-ups, it's just not fair.

With Céline, I know it is expensive. Half of the time I know where the fabric comes from and where it's made – and you know what – it is worth it. I would hope that people choose to buy expensive things because they know that they will be of value to them, and that they will be in their lives for a long time. Customers today are willing to pay for perfection.

With the market so saturated with designers and brands, luxury is becoming much more important. Where once a designer label would have sufficed, the customer today is far more discerning – willing to pay for perfection, but more demanding. As such, she has shifted her attention away from some of the usual suspects, preferring to spend not on the seasonal – on clothing that has a short life span – but on garments with integrity, with intricate details. Garments that are steeped in love and technique, that will stand the test of time.

Nowadays most designers do what amounts to couture pieces in their shows. But at the same time, some designers are also a bit afraid of the idea of couture because they think, shouldn't we be more modern? Should we be looking at the past? Should it be fantasy? Designers are afraid to show fantasy because they feel that the general public is looking in and thinking, this is not utilitarian enough, it isn't wearable enough. I can't get value for money out of this.

The very nature of fashion is that it is forever changing. But perhaps it is now evolving quicker than it should. Not that couture doesn't – but couture is never totally fashion. Couture is for special occasions, a fantasy born of a desire to be the best it possibly can be, both for the designer and for the client, and so the fashion element isn't always the main content or the reasoning behind it. It is an incubator for ideas that facilitate the content and raison d'être behind what is labelled as prêt-à-porter. If handled correctly, couture can also help promote a house, sell perfumes, accessories and prêt-à-porter, too. Couture is the ultimate in clothing and luxury, and its duty is to remain so.

Azzedine Alaïa may not appear on the couture schedule, but if ever there was a couturier, then it is him. I don't know anyone else today who can make such beautiful garments from start to finish. He is the designer's designer, the high priest of fashion, from tailoring to flou, knit to accessories. He is the person from whom I could learn everything that there is to know about the art, the technique and, ultimately, the finished garment. The late Joseph Ettedgui once told me that Mr Alaïa would collect couture to preserve and to learn, to cherish and to give back. What more of an icon could you possibly wish for?

I recently interviewed Mr Alaïa for a magazine; he is my idol. He took me around his studio and showed me the one-off pieces and the wedding dresses and everything. And you know he makes it all. He is the first one there in the morning and the last one there at night. He makes his patterns; he sews things together. Every piece of production that comes in, he goes through, he touches, he checks himself. He is the only designer I know that you can say – whatever you buy from him – he has touched it. He is the ultimate.

I also went to his show this season. I had never been to one before, and it had been my dream to go. There were about 10 people there including Grace Coddington, Suzy Menkes and Carla Sozzani. I felt like I shouldn't be there at all. And what came out was exactly what you would expect from Azzedine. The colours were maybe different, and certain techniques were different. But he always builds on his very distinctive style. And everyone said afterwards, "Oh my God, I want everything."

I remember when I had just started to work for John Galliano. All the girls in the office had gone to Joseph to buy an Alaïa body because they had just come in – it was the new thing – and they all came back with a body, a chocolate-brown knitted body. They all bought the same one – it had one button here, quite low – and everyone looked amazing. And I thought, oh my God, this is a designer who can make all these different women, with all these different body shapes, look incredible in the same garment.

I can also remember years ago when Joseph had this tweed jacket specially created by Azzedine for his Sloane Street store. And Joseph was there. And Azzedine was there. And I was looking at this jacket, and then I noticed the sleevehead and, really, it was amazing. And I just thought, how on earth can I compete when there is a designer around who can create something so perfect?

And Azzedine came over and said, "Do you like it?", and I was like, "Oh my God," mainly because it was Azzedine Alaïa. And then I said, "That sleevehead is perfection." And he was so pleased. "It took me six months to get that sleevehead, and you are the first person to notice," he said.

"To me, couture is the idea of hundreds of different pairs of hands touching something; pieces of fragile tulle being carefully stitched together"

You look at what he does – and, yes, ostensibly it is prêt-à-porter. But it's so much more than that. His pieces speak from the hanger. That has to be every designer's ultimate goal.

Christian Dior is the couturier who has had the most influence on fashion. Not only for the work he produced, which continues to uphold the tradition, but also for those other designers who have raised the standard in his name and for the house he founded – people like Yves Saint Laurent in particular. There is also, of course, Marc Bohan, Gianfranco Ferré and John Galliano. Galliano was born to be a couturier. The fantasy, the dreamscapes, the sense of history and the underlying femininity are what couture is about. John has made history and he continues to do so, always in such a sublime fashion.

On a different note, a nod to Charles Frederick Worth, the first couturier, who spent his youth in the house next door to my parents' house. And to Karl Lagerfeld, who has steered the house of Chanel with such modernity and forward thinking whilst remaining true to the spirit of its founder.

For fantasy couture, Hollywood costume designer Jean Louis deserves a special mention. He created the black sheath dress that Rita Hayworth wore in *Gilda* – it would still fit into anyone's wardrobe now. And have you seen the outfits he did for Marlene Dietrich – the ones where she looks as though she is naked, with crystals all over her body? Dietrich did a tour in the 1970s, and Jean Louis did these dresses then, too. He has inspired everyone, including John at Dior. He started with a layer of tulle or chiffon on a base of flesh-coloured foam – and the tulle was then embroidered with hundreds of crystal beads. The dresses were hand-sewn onto her every night, and they looked incredibly sexy. Essentially, this is couture. And this is what

I love the most about it – all the work of the *petites mains* to create a barely there structure, invisible corsetry, the soft-as-cloud dresses that appear to defy the laws of gravity. That is magic. That is Cinderella time.

Couture has always been about fantasy. It's about making the most impossible things exist in the world. I can understand that designers are afraid that they will look old if they adopt that attitude. We think of couture as all those amazing evening gowns and ball gowns from old movies. I could just about argue that I make couture in the old sense of the word when I make a wedding dress. It is made to measure. The bride comes for fittings. But I don't really consider it couture. To me, couture is the idea of hundreds of different pairs of hands touching something; pieces of fragile tulle being carefully stitched together; invisible corsetry; the most stunning beadwork or the most amazing featherwork. That, to me, is couture. It has to be a dream. It has to be like an artist creating a piece of work, and you look at it and think to yourself, yup, I could never do that.

"Couture is about making the most impossible things exist in the world"

Biographical Notes

Antonio Berardi was born in 1968 in Grantham after his parents had moved to England from Sicily in the 1950s.

He studied at Central Saint Martins and worked as John Galliano's assistant. In 1994, he started his own label. Kylie Minogue modelled for his first official show in 1995; the collection was immediately snapped up by buyers.

Berardi's signature body-conscious designs include tailored leather trouser suits, sheer chiffon dresses that are often embellished with crystals, and hand-painted flower patterns. Eva Mendes, Victoria Beckham and Penélope Cruz have all worn his designs; Gwyneth Paltrow memorably wore his risqué, see-through lace dress at the French premiere of *Two Lovers* in 2008.

In September 2009, Berardi returned to show at London Fashion Week after several years showing in Milan and Paris.

He designed a corset exclusively for Sarah Jessica Parker, which she wore on *The Late Show with David Letterman* in December 2009, and his chain-mail cocktail dress featured in 2010's *Sex and the City 2*.

Thom Browne

CAN I PREFACE ALL OF MY THOUGHTS on couture with the understanding that I am not, by far, an expert on the history of fashion? That said, the sensibilities back in the '50s – and what Christian Dior was doing then – that's where I start out when I design. He took something classic and very good-looking, and made it not so very classic and sometimes not so good-looking. That's why what he did has always been interesting to me, in terms of the quality and the details from the late '40s and early '50s. I can't say one outfit has totally inspired me beyond all others; it's more the classical sensibility that drives me, as I'm sure it drove him. Does that sound as though I'm giving myself credit? I'm not.

One of my biggest influences is looking through old couture books. For me, fashion is very much about the quality of how things are made, and the attention to detail. So my introduction to couture was through looking at old pictures of Dior, Givenchy and Balenciaga. And it's far less to do with embellishment and far more to do with construction. After you construct something, you can choose to embellish it. But what counts in true couture is the quality and how it is made. Although not strictly a couturier, Rei Kawakubo is one of the most influential designers of the past 100 years. It would be interesting to see what she would do with true couture. She's so strict in regard to attention to detail and construction, and her knowledge of tailoring is such that I'm sure many people would call her a couturier.

I don't get inspired by other people's work to the point that I wish I had designed any one outfit of anyone else's. Once something is done, it's done. I might think, wow, that's amazing, but I wouldn't wish I had done it. There's no reason for wishing I had done it. I deliberately don't pay any attention to fashion in the way that some designers do. I think that not knowing what's going on is easier, and allows me to get on and do my own thing. I think that, really, ignorance is bliss. I feel we should all just pay attention to what we are doing.

The most interesting thing about couture is the marriage of fantasy and craft. This is what separates fashion design from couture. The attention to construction is the most important thing. It's very easy to jerry-rig something together and for it to be nice. But to create something that's very seriously made, and beautifully fantastic – that's what makes all the difference. That's what is most important.

I've been lucky enough to learn my trade from one of the best tailors in the world. He is just brilliant. The great thing about Rocco Ciccarelli is that he came to the States from Rome in the

"Karl has really taken what Chanel was and made it his own, but you can still feel what it was. I still feel the old Chanel. In fact, I love the old Chanel. There was a really beautiful unovert sexiness about it"

'50s. He talks about tailoring back then, and describes it as the best in the world, because it was a combination of Italian, French and American tailoring. There were so many skilled people coming to the US and working together as tailors that, between them, they developed a new American aesthetic. People appreciated that back then. They are starting to again now. But in the '70s, '80s and '90s, it got lost somewhere. I haven't learned everything yet. I learn every day. I would never claim to be an expert on any of that.

To be in fashion, you have to really love it. You can't do it just for the money. It's a lot of work. You have to be serious about wanting to create fashion and not be seduced by the world surrounding fashion. The best bit for me is being in my factory in Long Island City – really glamorous! It's pretty down and dirty. Sometimes mystery is better than the reality.

I think many couture designers continue to influence us today. Galliano, for example, influences us through his showmanship – well, the marriage of quality and showmanship.

I think Christian Lacroix was the perfect combination of fantasy and actual wearability; you could easily imagine people wearing his clothes. I would put Rei in this group, just because of the importance of what she contributes to fashion. And, of course, Karl Lagerfeld for his ability to shape the commerce of couture. His shows are always so beautiful. You can actually see how he has managed to embody the world of Coco Chanel in every collection.

I think it must be difficult to take over a fashion house that has a very distinctive aesthetic, like Chanel. I would guess that it depends on how you start out. Galliano, for example, has created a whole new world for Dior and, while I'm sure that he respects wholeheartedly what the Dior house originally was, I think it is very different now to what it was. I think that Karl has really taken what Chanel was and made it his own, but you can still feel what it was. I still feel the old Chanel. In fact, I love the old Chanel. There was a really beautiful unovert sexiness about it, just in the proportions. Now it's a lot sexier. I'm of the school of "less is more".

The great lesson we can learn from couture is how much the skilled "hands" were appreciated. Valentino, for example, had incredible respect for the people who worked for him. You can tell from the documentary about him, *The Last Emperor*, how very much he appreciated the ladies in his atelier. That, for me, was what was so lovely about that documentary. You could tell that the relationship between them all was really beautiful. I think we all now sit back and think in a far more commercial way and, you know, that's what really ruins it. Because these days,

Above: A Cristóbal Balenciaga asymmetrically fastening suit in dog-tooth check with patch pockets at the hip and three-quarter-length sleeves

Left: Givenchy's culotte suit – in dark green and purple – caused a sensation when it was first shown in Paris in 1967. The slim-fitting jacket is worn over culottes cut to below the knee. The matching top coat has a military-style collar. The outfit is completed by a green felt hat and long patent boots

Opposite: Thom Browne's Spring/Summer 2011 show opened with the models dressed as astronauts before they disrobed into a series of suits displaying the cropped aesthetic for which Browne has become known. Shark and goldfish motifs featured alongside contemporary stripes, trousers cut above the knee, sleeves falling shy of the wrist – and plenty of gold lipstick

you do have to find a balance between how much you have to compromise your ideals and how much you don't. It's not always easy.

There are certain designers who treat couture in a fantasy way, and I love that. It opens people's eyes and makes them think differently. I would personally never show something that was almost costume-unwearable. Everything I do, I could see someone wearing – except for maybe my three-legged trouser. But that was really done to prove that we could make something mad but take it just as seriously as a classic trouser. That was the reason for that trouser. Plus, the show was staged in a circus. Despite what some people say, I always find Christian Lacroix's couture very wearable; I could see all of what he does being worn, but maybe I have a bizarre mind – which is always a good thing.

> "Everything I do, I could see someone wearing – except for maybe my three-legged trouser"

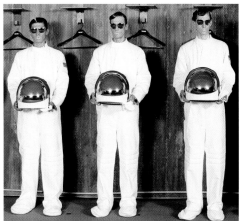

Biographical Notes

Thom Browne was born in 1965 and grew up in Pennsylvania. He studied economics at the University of Notre Dame in Indiana, then briefly attempted an acting career in Los Angeles before moving to New York in 1997, where he worked as a salesman in Giorgio Armani's showroom. His interest in fashion began as a hobby and stemmed from his love of vintage clothing, which he wore around LA for fun.

He debuted the Thom Browne collection in 2001 with no formal fashion training; since he couldn't afford to manufacture a full collection, he made five suits and wore them around town, asking friends to buy them from him. He created his collection with the help of Rocco Ciccarelli, an Italian menswear tailor with 60 years' experience.

Browne has become known for shrunken, ankle-baring suits that are smart but have a boyish flair, as well as for his theatrical runway shows. He won the Council of Fashion Designers of America award for Menswear Designer of the Year in 2006 and *GQ* Designer of the Year in 2008. Since 2008, Browne has designed a range of men's sportswear for Moncler called Moncler Gamme Bleu, and in June 2010 he announced he would create his first full line of womenswear.

The House of Christian Dior

The name Christian Dior is synonymous with pure elegance and sheer romance. Since the launch of the Corolle collection – better known as the New Look – in 1947, the House of Dior has set the trends of the season and set the bar for sculpted structure and extravagant embellishment. Since John Galliano's arrival in 1996, the house has rediscovered a reputation for inspiration and won the hearts of the world's fashion elite.

"At the risk of being thought soulless, and in spite of my love of architecture and interior decoration, I must admit that clothes are my whole life. Ultimately everything I know, see or hear, every part of my life, turns around the clothes which I create. They haunt me perpetually, until they are ready to pass from the world of my dreams into the world of practical utility"

Christian Dior

1905: Christian Dior is born in Granville, in Normandy, France.

1928: After abandoning his political studies, Dior opens an art gallery in Paris funded by his father. He is part of a Bohemian set that includes Christian Bérard and Jean Cocteau.

1935: After Dior's family falls on hard times, Dior begins sketching designs for a number of fashion houses.

1938: Dior joins Robert Piguet as a designer.

1942: Dior joins Lucien Lelong, where he works alongside Pierre Balmain.

1945: Balmain leaves to set up his own couture house.

1946: Dior approaches an entrepreneur/cotton magnate for funding to set up his own couture house. Marcel Boussac, head of Comptoir de l'Industrie Cotonnière, sets up Dior in a Parisian townhouse mansion at 30 Avenue Montaigne.

1947: Dior launches his fashion house with the Corolle collection, which is quickly nicknamed the New Look by the press. Tiny, corseted waists, accentuated hips, full skirts and luxe fabrics – epitomised by the iconic Bar suit – become an overnight sensation. On 27th March, *Life* magazine reports, "Last month Paris fashion got a much-needed shot in the arm. Making his first appearance as an independent couturier, a middle-aged ex-art dealer named Christian Dior brought out a collection of 94 evening gowns, dresses and suits, which sent buyers racing to the fitting rooms to get their orders in first, even before the show was over."

In the context of post-war, strike-weary Paris, the collection is repudiated by a certain class of Parisian women who feel that the ostentatious designs are a provocation.

Yves Saint Laurent's Trapeze collection for Dior

Dior with a model for his 1948 Envol collection

Mark Bohan at Dior, 1970

Dior travels to the US to roll out the collection to Americans. In Chicago he is met by women with banners saying, "Down with the New Look". Nevertheless, the collections are an international success.

1948: The Envol collection of scooped skirts and fly-back jackets is embraced by a converted public.

1949: Slim skirts and bloused bodices herald a new silhouette and earn Dior the nickname "Dictator", because women are forced to completely change their wardrobe each season.

1950: Marlene Dietrich wears a number of dresses designed by Dior in the Alfred Hitchcock film *Stage Fright*.

1953: Barrel-shaped coats worn over shorter skirts create a softer, more accessible look that remains popular throughout the '50s.

1955: A quiet young Yves Mathieu-Saint-Laurent joins the Dior house as a design assistant.

1957: Dior's last collection includes chemise dresses and tunics, Breton-style smocks with stand-away collars and patch pockets, and khaki bush jackets. After the collection, Dior dies suddenly of a heart attack. The unknown Yves Saint Laurent, aged 21, is appointed his successor.

1958: Saint Laurent launches the Trapeze collection to rapturous acclaim. He cleverly combines his own love of a more fluid, relaxed form with the house's signature romantic, opulent aesthetic.

1960: Saint Laurent is called up for military service. When he is released, he discovers that Marc Bohan has replaced him as Artistic Director.

1961: Bohan's collection is deemed a success, and Elizabeth Taylor orders 12 dresses.

1989: Gianfranco Ferré replaces Bohan and is named design director for women's ready-to-wear, couture and accessories.

1996: A new golden age of haute couture is launched by the arrival of Dior's new designer, John Galliano. Princess Diana wears a Galliano dress at the opening of the Metropolitan Museum of Art's 50-year Dior retrospective exhibition.

1997: In January, at the Grand Hotel in Paris, Galliano reinvents the world of haute couture by drawing on the sort of inspirations that Dior himself may well have adopted. The press consensus is that Galliano has found his spiritual home.

2007: The House of Dior celebrates its 60th anniversary with a show and a star-studded party at Versailles attended by Naomi Campbell, Jessica Alba, Kate Hudson and Charlize Theron.

2010: Galliano's Autumn/Winter couture collection is a paean to all things floral. The finale gowns, with vast, petal-shaped full skirts, reflect the romance and extravagance of Dior's first Corolle collection. Galliano is lauded for his continuing inspiration and audacity.

"The most important couturier ever? Christian Dior for making the world look new"
John Galliano

Gianfranco Ferré at Dior, Spring/Summer 1992

John Galliano's first collection for Dior, 1997

Galliano on the runway in 2010

MY SISTER USED TO GIVE ME all her old copies of *The Face* and *i-D*. I suppose that's what set me on the road to a career in fashion. I also had an aunt who was a model in the '60s, so fashion was always very much part of my background. My family was into the whole Biba thing, and was always looking at fashion anyway. But my first real experience of couture happened when I was about 15.

I used to visit the V&A on school art trips. We used to get carted out to lots of different places. One time we were just doing a general trip to the V&A, and there happened to be an exhibition of couture. I think it was different couturiers throughout the 20th century – probably from their archive. I can remember being amazed by the work that goes into couture fashion. I'm one of those people who naturally gravitates towards the most expensive things in life, and that's what happened at that exhibition. I became really interested in couture, because I could see that, judging by the amount of detail, it was the world's best fashion. I later realised that couture is so much more impressive when it's worn and there's movement.

I still find it interesting looking at couturiers' work. There was a lot of diversity in Balenciaga's original work. Looking at it in person is a rare experience, but when I do, I get a feeling – there's something about it, I can't describe it. It just feels right. There are some things that just feel inherently right and I don't know why. His treatment of fabric – the way it's cut – is genius. There's one Balenciaga jacket – it's in a black-and-white photo – you can just tell how amazingly it's made. The detail and precision in the panels are a great example of how something two-dimensional, a sketch or a flat pattern, can be brought to life so perfectly on the body.

Chanel should be credited with changing the way women dress. It was during the Belle Époque when women were corseted and wearing very strict, tight clothes that Chanel started transferring ideas that she found in menswear into womenswear. She gave women the ease and comfort that they hadn't experienced before. It's such a modern idea, even today. I suppose today women go out in a pair of very high heels; that must be pretty uncomfortable. But back then, every single item in a woman's wardrobe was restrictive in some way. Chanel freed up womenswear. She used amazing couture techniques, and often incredibly feminine finishes, but on garments that were much more modern in those times. Chanel foresaw the future of womenswear.

Christian Dior, of course, brought back corsetry in 1947 with the New Look – but it was corseted in a different way. It was about showing off

Kim Jones
Dunhill

"I love frivolity; I love high fashion. But I also love really good, quality things. If you're going to invest, you want to be able to wear the garment; it needs to have a purpose"

a woman's figure. It redefined the silhouette. I always love to look at fashion in terms of the peaks and troughs of the economy, which always reflect in the way that people dress. In the good times, people get freed up. Post-war, people wanted to celebrate the end of austerity. It was a social thing rather than merely a fashion thing. People wanted to show off their money, but not in a vulgar way. They enjoyed beautifully crafted clothes and full-on glamour.

The real collectors of couture, like Nan Kempner, have all gone. Now when people have money, they tend to show off their wealth on obvious spectacular pieces. I think it is far more sophisticated to spend money on clothes that will last a long time. Listen, I love frivolity; I love high fashion. But I also love really good, quality things. If you're going to invest, you want to be able to wear the garment; it needs to have a purpose.

Today, Chanel is probably the most relevant couture house. The other fashion houses simply use couture as a precursor to what the next ready-to-wear collection will be about. I look at couture for that kind of inspiration, too. But Chanel is different. I like the quietness of it rather than the loudness. Chanel has clothes for women who want to buy couture. Karl Lagerfeld has maintained its original principles in the most successful way. I mean, I love Dior as a showcase of experimental, amazing fashions. But I was in the Wolseley having lunch the other day, and there was this woman wearing haute couture Chanel, and you knew what it was, immediately. Chanel is still part of the real world. It's not just for a big ball or a black-tie event. It can do lunch. If you're going to spend £10K on an outfit, you want to be able to wear it more than once. I watched an amazing documentary, *The Secret World of Haute Couture*. In it, Betsy Bloomingdale revealed that she wrote on a card for each dress the dates she wore it and where she wore it, so she knew exactly how many times it had been worn and for what – and each dress then became part of the family history.

Real collectors of couture have a lot of attachment to their clothes. There's a certain level of wealth where things get passed down from one generation to the next. You get your mother's Chanel suit or your grandfather's Savile Row jacket, and you might wear it in a completely new way. Giving something new life is fantastic. At Dunhill, I make a real effort to ensure that my designs will transcend the generations so that they can become heirlooms.

I've never really worked on couture. But Lee McQueen was a really good friend, and I used to watch him doing stuff. He knew how to make the most of those intricate techniques.

Seeing Lee make special one-off showpieces that had so much energy in them – that was like watching art happen. These days, couture has become a seedbed for ideas. It gets people thinking outside the box. The most exciting new ideas come from womenswear. And within that, the most exciting new ideas come from those houses that also do couture. They have the time and freedom to make things beyond the normal realms of fashion. You can try things out that might cost £15K to make, but you can do that. Outside of couture, there's a lot of financial restriction on creativity. Couture is fashion in its most extravagant form.

Who would I like to have worked for? It's a hard question, as I've been fortunate enough to work with some great people. But Dior and Chanel both spring to mind because of the way they reinvented the looks of the time. Both of them created a new silhouette. I love reinvention. I love rebranding. To be at the forefront of something is so exciting. I look at the archives, but I'm much more into looking outside the box rather than inside it. It's very easy to slip into nostalgia. You have to be forward-thinking. I like the essence of the old world, but within the new world.

Biographical Notes

Dunhill was founded in London in 1893 when Alfred Dunhill took over his father's saddlery business. Today, the brand specialises in men's clothing, accessories, writing instruments, fragrances and luxury goods.

London-born Kim Jones was accepted into Central Saint Martins without any previous fashion training. Jones presented his first catwalk collection for London Fashion Week in September 2003 and made his Paris debut in July 2004. Jones also art-directed for *Dazed & Confused*, *Arena Homme Plus*, *Numero Homme*, *Another Magazine* and *Ten*.

Jones was named Menswear Designer of the Year by the British Fashion Council in 2006, and again in 2009.

Jones was appointed Creative Director at Dunhill in March 2008, presenting his first collection for Dunhill in 2009. He has embraced Dunhill's rich archives, putting a modern spin on the traditional heritage. His Autumn/Winter 2010 collection was inspired by a photo journal made by Clement Court, who was manager of Dunhill's French business back in the 1920s. The pictures marked the journey from Paris to Japan, via Mongolia, Siberia, Korea and Russia. The collection was a mix of British-looking suits mixed with cashmere knits and heavy wool outerwear.

Left: A Cristóbal Balenciaga jacket photographed in September 1951 by Henry Clarke for French Vogue, and displaying the couturier's precision cutting and attention to detail. Cecil Beaton dubbed him "the Picasso of fashion"

Below left: Looks from Christian Dior, October 1950

Below right: Models in tweed suits by Coco Chanel, photographed for Life magazine by Paul Schutzer in Paris, 1961. Chanel first created the iconic two-piece tweed suit in 1928 – around the same time as the little black dress first appeared

Opposite: Kim Jones' Spring/Summer 2011 collection for Dunhill harks back to '20s and '30s English Modernism – in particular the Bloomsbury Group. The key jacket of the collection – a softly tailored, high-fastening double-breasted blazer with a single set of buttons and flared silhouette (main picture) – was inspired by pieces worn by Bloomsbury Group members John Maynard Keynes and Roger Fry

THERE WERE TWO THINGS that sparked my career in fashion: the first one was Tim Blanks on *Fashion File*; the second was Canal Cinq – Channel 5 – which was the big channel when I was growing up in Montreal. It's the French channel. They would report during Couture Week on the normal six o'clock news – which is so lovely and French; no other country would consider couture to be news. That was my introduction to fashion. I was about 13. *Fashion File* reported all the shows. I remember all the Chanel shows with Karl Lagerfeld, and even things like Galliano when he did the Russian Princess collection, which was one of his first. And all the amazing Dior shows. And then Tim Blanks standing in front of the Tuileries saying, "This is Tim Blanks reporting for *Fashion File*!" I know him now. He's really nice.

Yves Saint Laurent is the most inspirational designer – the designer of so many firsts. He was the first designer to put black models on the catwalk and the first to make ready-to-wear relevant; he's an icon in the truest sense. When you consider that he was thrust into the position of head of Dior at the tender age of 21 – he was incredible from the start. In terms of couture, he was a voyager – he would travel and take you with him – and he was a great colourist.

Christian Lacroix is also an amazing colourist. Actually, he is probably my favourite. I wonder if I should have said him first. I guess I would say they are both the most inspirational. If it's who is the most influential designer in the world, in general, I think Yves Saint Laurent. The structure that he put into place has probably had the most influence on how fashion works today. And he was a very real proposition for his clients. I reckon he was designing for specific women that he knew, as much as he was dreaming.

Then there's also the contrasting colours and cultures and textiles of Christian Lacroix. He realised a fantasy dream. It's fashion in the form of ecstasy. It's fashion in its purest form.

In terms of historical influence, Dior and Chanel were both a liberating force in their own ways. Chanel changed how women wore clothes, so I guess that she has had the most influence. She freed up women's fashion and created a totally timeless aesthetic. She did away with the corset, dropped waistlines, and introduced *la garçonne* – fabulous. I almost feel, though, that Dior liberated women too – in a different sense. He offered luxury, post-war. Suddenly he introduced the idea of nipped-in waists, huge amounts of fabric and luxe. I suppose it was a reintroduction of luxury. But isn't that a form of liberation? Maybe, in a weird way, it was a licence for women to dress up again.

It is human nature to always want and need

Erdem Moralioglu
Erdem

"If I could have designed a garment from couture history, it would be anything from Yves Saint Laurent's first collection for Dior. I don't mind which – anything at all. The Trapeze collection was incredible"

the best. Luxury will always be desirable. Does couture have a future? I worry sometimes that the client base is shrinking. It seems to go in shifts, geographically. Sometimes it's all American clients; at others it's all Chinese clients. But couture has always evolved.

When you think about the '80s – and houses like Yves Saint Laurent, Lacroix, Patou, and Chanel – it was a time of huge wealth, and I guess all that wealth added up to a period of distinct excess, of increased fantasy. Not that the period was any more important in cultural terms than other periods – it just stands out as a point in time when couture changed.

If I could have designed a garment from couture history, it would be anything from Yves Saint Laurent's first collection for Dior. I don't mind which – anything at all. The Trapeze collection was incredible. If I could have worked for any of them, I would choose Charles James for cutting, Yves Saint Laurent for colour, and Balenciaga for everything. And Karl Lagerfeld. I mean, he's amazing; he's a real couturier. He's our modern couturier. I should have said him earlier, shouldn't I? He has retained Chanel's vision and simultaneously introduced a sense of humour, which is brilliant. I adore him for his astuteness, his modernity and his total chicness.

Of all the couture techniques, embroidery has always attracted me. The idea of manipulating textiles by depth, by weight and by hand is fascinating. If you look at the collections by houses like Chanel, where they still use the work of Lesage and the feather supplier Lemarié – these ateliers – Chanel in particular has kept them going. I went to Lesage once. I was in the third year of my BA at a very small college in Canada, and I entered a worldwide competition to design eveningwear, and we won. One of the prizes was a visit to the Lacroix fashion house, and we all got sent over to Paris; it was amazing. I got a tour of Lacroix's couture house, where he invites all the clients. And the ladies that worked for him rolled out the collection. It was the collection that Alek Wek modelled, and it was kind of long, quilted bomber jackets with gold Lesage embroideries down the shoulders. They were fabulous. The moment I set foot into his atelier, that clinched it for me.

If I'm honest, I have always been into fashion – even before Tim Blanks appeared on my TV. It's quite embarrassing, but I'll say it anyway: I remember being about six, and my parents took me to *The Nutcracker*, and when I got home I made a paper doll chain of every single costume. I was shocked – pleasantly so – by the way they were all dressed up. That's probably what sealed the deal. I was very young. The first dress I ever made was for my twin sister's Barbie.

It was a circle skirt with a bodice, powder blue and strapless. My sister was very pleased. I've made her many clothes since – my sister, that is.

Couture means to create by hand. It is a balance between a dream and a service. I think that couture should have a certain *joie de vivre*, but it's not really fashion in its purest form. I think that fashion in its purest form exists all around us. There is no difference between the way a 14-year-old girl throws on a sweatshirt and how her mother wears her Chanel couture jacket. Fashion is simply an expression.

> "Couture is a balance between a dream and a service. I think it should have a certain *joie de vivre*, but it's not really fashion in its purest form"

Biographical Notes

Erdem Moralioglu was born in 1976 in Montreal, Canada to an English mother and Turkish father.

In 2000 he moved to London to study for a Masters degree in fashion at the Royal College of Art. He then went on to work for Diane von Furstenberg in New York, before returning to London and setting up his own label. In September 2005, he won the Fashion Fringe competition, which nurtures undiscovered design talent, and established his eponymous ready-to-wear line of vibrant abstract prints and romantic, delicate dresses.

He caught the public's attention when Claudia Schiffer wore one of his designs to the 2006 BAFTAs. His celebrity fans include Thandie Newton, Sienna Miller, Keira Knightley, Tilda Swinton and Michelle Obama.

He has received a number of awards, including the 2007 Swarovski British Fashion Council Fashion Enterprise award; the British Fashion Council's 2008 Fashion Forward award; the 2009 Fashion Future award at the *Elle* Style Awards; and in 2010 he won the inaugural BFC/*Vogue* Fashion Fund award, worth £200,000. His Autumn/Winter 2009 show was listed as one of Style.com's top 10 shows of the season. He was also nominated for the British Fashion Council's 2009 Collection of the Year Award for his bold use of colour and print.

Opposite: Designs from Erdem's ready-to-wear Autumn/Winter 2010 collection were inspired by his twin sister's teenage wardrobe, nature documentaries, their childhood in Quebec, and the lost schoolgirls in the film 'Picnic at Hanging Rock' (1975). The collection includes high-necked short dresses, bias-cut blouses and floor-trailing gowns in lace and silk. Moralioglu's trademark colour-clashing prints are nature-inspired, with the motif of a swallow on a stormy sky appearing throughout

Right: Christian Lacroix's skills as a colourist and his knowledge of historical costume – especially that of 18th-century French painting – is demonstrated by this strapless evening gown from his Spring/Summer 1990 collection, a riot of Mediterranean colours

Above: Yves Saint Laurent's red Sailor dress from his Spring/Summer 1958 Trapeze line for Dior. Saint Laurent's highly successful first collection featured his new triangular shape, gently flaring from narrow shoulders to a short, wide hemline just covering the knees. By autumn 1958, all of Paris was wearing this dress shape. The full, box-pleated raw silk skirt over organdie petticoats is worn with a middy sailor jacket with a bow, and a matching flat-stitched sailor hat

Wes Gordon

MY FIRST EXPERIENCE OF COUTURE was when I was an intern. I was in this vintage fashion retail store. They have these places here in New York, hidden up in buildings – the sorts of places that stylists go to borrow vintage stuff for shoots and things. I was with a girl doing research on accessories, and I wandered off on my own. And I found this amazing pleated Madame Grès gown with all the little tucks and things. I put my hands right around it. And the tightest you could get it was like this, because there was so much fabric in it. I vividly remember that. It was matte silk jersey. And it was all done by hand. Incredible workmanship. I probably wasn't meant to do that, was I?

I think Galliano and Lagerfeld are the two true ends of the couture spectrum, and all the others basically fall in between. I always watch those two first on Style.com. Chanel is always beautiful and fantasy and fun. But it's not complete frivolity. It's also "real clothes" that real women buy. There is a place in couture for frivolity – I'm not saying otherwise. But there are women out there who are actually wearing Chanel couture. Couture is theatre. It's amazing theatre, but when you have someone actually wearing the outfit, it makes it all the more relevant.

Galliano is at the other end of the spectrum; he's a genius. He's the reason that I went to Central Saint Martins. It's so much fun – the hair and the make-up and everything. You have to wonder how one person can come up with all that. A girlfriend of mine at Saint Martins – her mum bought some of Galliano's first collection, and they ended up in her dressing-up box. She'd play at dressing up in the Incroyable collection from 1984, and his name was in the back, and everything.

When I was a kid in Atlanta, I used to take lessons with this Russian couturier. She had a couture house in the Soviet Union and then she came over to America and set up an alterations shop. I used to go to her for lessons in pattern cutting and hand-sewing, things like that. She used to make me sew lines on lined paper. You know, like follow the blue lines exactly. She would get very mad if I went off the lines. It wasn't Chanel couture, but it was the same atmosphere of perfectionism.

I wish I could have designed anything by Balenciaga. Or the original Halston clothes. A vintage Halston dress is, like, genius. It has the same idea as Balenciaga – great fluidity, just a few seams, a great cut. Combined with American sportswear. Every time I see a vintage Halston I think, ugh, I can't believe he beat me to it.

In terms of real couture – I have visited Valentino in Milan. I had an interview there once when I was still at Saint Martins. I love, love, love old Valentino. It's sad that he has retired. But I guess things move on. The dress that Julia Roberts wore – the black-and-white vintage one. That's the best. He's a real inspiration.

I don't think I'll ever do a collection of gowns like Valentino, but there's something undeniably amazing about '70s or '80s Valentino. You see those images of a woman in the middle of a room wearing one of those gowns, and it's just amazing. If I could translate that kind of idea to a great jacket or coat, then that is much more interesting to me.

Dior has had the most profound influence on fashion history. You read about the New Look in school history books, which is a pretty rare thing for a fashion collection. He transformed the whole mind-set of women on how they wore clothes. They went from frugality and practicality to complete fantasy. Would we have approved of it at the time? I think deep down I'm a minimalist, so I may have been saying, "You don't need 40 metres of chiffon to do what you can with two".

I wonder if people are more interested in the spectacle of couture rather than the quality of it. Everyone is after the Lady Gaga factor. It's probably just because 99.9% of people only see couture as an image – a picture in a magazine or on Style.com. The construction is only really appreciated by the people who wear it, and they are becoming fewer and fewer.

The terms "couture" or "ready-to-wear" are increasingly irrelevant for some designers. Oscar de la Renta is a good example of this, and Christophe Decarnin at Balmain. Both of them create ready-to-wear that could easily cross over into the couture bracket in terms of price. You could go to designers who call themselves couturiers and find something for less. And it's the same in American stores. You find designs in the contemporary department and the designer department that overlap in price. It's a free-for-all now – so very different from the past.

I once saw a documentary about Yves Saint Laurent that showed the lead-up to his last couture show. There were incredibly gorgeous women everywhere. There were bolts of fabulous fabric stacked up against the walls, dozens of seamstresses creating the most beautiful voile creations for his inspection. And his little dog was running all over the place. Couture is a secret world. Nothing like it exists anywhere else. Can you imagine experiencing real couture like that first-hand? For an overall experience, you can't get much better than that.

I could learn so much from Karl Lagerfeld, but it would be the scariest place in the world to work, wouldn't it? Did you see that bit in the Valentino documentary when Lagerfeld said that they were the only two people in the world

"I wish I could have designed anything by Balenciaga. Or the original Halston clothes. A vintage Halston dress is, like, genius"

"To own something that no one else does, that has taken weeks to create by hand, that's beautiful – that is the ultimate. Couture is the ultimate luxury"

Above: A still from 'Yves Saint Laurent: 5 avenue Marceau 75116 Paris' by David Teboul. The film takes a behind-the-scenes look at the creation of Yves Saint Laurent's last collection in January 2002

Below left: A close-up of Yves Saint Laurent's muse, Loulou de la Falaise, smoking through the veil of her black hat. She was the inspiration for his Le Smoking jacket. The photograph was taken for American Vogue, January 1969

Far left: Yves Saint Laurent's muse, actress Catherine Deneuve, being fitted at Saint Laurent's atelier in the 1970s

Opposite: From Wes Gordon's Autumn/ Winter 2010 debut womenswear collection. Inspired by Lauren Bacall, the collection included tailored separates such as this double-breasted leather jacket (bottom left) and pussy-bow cashmere coat with leather sleeves and fox-fur cuffs

to make fashion? That was quite a statement. I would judge Yves Saint Laurent, Lagerfeld, Valentino and Oscar de le Renta as the pinnacle of fashion. I would definitely include Oscar in that group. He's a genius. And I really admire Armani and Ralph.

In my own collection, the pieces that really worked – and by worked I mean sold well – are the ones that had something different about them. The special pieces. It wasn't particularly a price issue at all. I had gone into the design of the collection thinking, I've gotta have some entry-level pieces. But I think that, at a higher price point, people look for something a bit different, something fun. The pieces that had pleats or leather or embroidery sold well. So there goes my minimal aesthetic. It's minimal with a grain of salt.

There are what – seven billion people in the world? And everyone wants to feel special. It's easy to forget that. Everything is mass-produced. You only have to get on a subway in New York and within five seconds you will no longer feel special. Luxury in its purest form has the magic of reminding you that you're special. To own something that no one else does, that has taken weeks to create by hand, that's beautiful – that is the ultimate. Couture is the ultimate luxury; it's there to make us dream. All beautiful clothes, whether couture or ready-to-wear, are there to make us dream. Perhaps, though, with couture, the dreams are more dramatic.

Biographical Notes

Wes Gordon was born in Atlanta, Georgia. He took a BA in Fashion Womenswear at Central Saint Martins and graduated in 2009. His graduate collection, called the Glass Collection, incorporated glass blown into a bodice, epaulettes and collars. He formed an early clientele by making dresses for girls he met on the social scene. He also worked as an intern at Oscar de la Renta and Tom Ford.

Gordon was just 23 when he presented his first collection at New York Fashion Week in February 2010; the collection featured jackets that blended wool, leather and panels of beaded chiffon. He won the Jenny Packham Bursary for Design and Excellence. He was invited to participate in the first Blueprint Fashion Show in Singapore, a three-day show designed to bridge the gap between East and West.

His style icons include Kate Moss, Carla Bruni, Cate Blanchett, Daphne Guinness and Kate Beckinsale. His designs have appeared in *The New York Times*, *Women's Wear Daily* and *Vogue*.

Stephen Jones

I'D LOVE TO BE ABLE TO SAY that my earliest experience of couture was aged four with mummy's ball gown or something. But it was much later in life. The first time I walked into the workroom at Givenchy, John Galliano said to me, "Stephen, this is Marie-Beatrice, and she will be the head of your workroom." That was it. It was a dream come true. I was the first British person to work in a couture millinery workroom. There was extraordinary lineage there and fantastic techniques. It was a huge privilege and massively exciting. Total terror as well, because you think of all these wonderful hats that had been created in there. All the hats for Audrey Hepburn, all the hats from *Funny Face* were made in this workroom – and then I'm asking these people to make my hats!

In the millinery workshop of an haute couture house, all the workers wear white coats. I actually don't wear one, and they all think it's hilarious and revolutionary that I don't. I always wear an apron – a blue and white striped butcher's apron – and everybody always falls about and asks me for a pound of sausages. It's good because it's very long and it has a huge pocket in the front that I can keep all my rubbish in, like my scissors.

Every milliner in the atelier has a different personality, a different character, and will produce different hats. Haute couture is personal not only to the person wearing it but also to the person making it. It's the same as a piano recital. If you imagine the audience is the person wearing couture, then the musician playing the solo is the couturier. The person who makes, say, a suit, has a huge influence on what it ends up looking like. For example, if I am working in my Dior workroom – as I am at the moment – if I have something that is a strict felt to do, I would give it to Maria. But if I have drapery to do, I will give it to Silvana. Silvana can't do the felt with absolute precision and Maria gets terrified by drapery because it needs supreme confidence. I remember once asking Silvana why she was so good at drapery, and she answered, "Because I am Parisian." *Et voilà* – the most fantastic reply. You have to have total confidence at being Parisian, and having those techniques, which have been handed down over hundreds of years, to be able to say something like that. They start when they're 16; they go to a special school to learn it.

Sometimes a hat may move through different people. Of course, even though we say this person should be making this and this person should be making that – that's only in an ideal world. When all the fabrics arrive only three days before the show, it's all hands on deck. We get everybody, including the receptionist, to help.

My favourite couturier in history is Schiaparelli. She combined art and fashion. She also made fantastic hats. She saw clothes as entertainment,

which is how I see fashion. The most influential designer would be Christian Dior because of what he achieved. His 1947 collection completely mirrored what the public wanted – even though they didn't know it. It was extraordinary because of that. In the same way that punk had reality because there was a social movement to go with it, the New Look was about romance and fantasy after women had been wearing military-style clothing during and since the war.

There are two designers that I wish I could have worked for: Jacques Fath in the late '40s and '50s, because he made clothes that were so glamorous, and hats that were very good too – I would have loved to have had a stab at them; and Balenciaga in the early '60s. He did really wonderful, extraordinarily crazy hats. The one hat I wish I had designed? Yes, of course, the shoe hat by Schiaparelli.

John Galliano continues to inspire me today. He brings excitement, fantasy and beautiful clothes to the world. Somehow, John has reinvented haute couture, but I don't think that was his purpose. I think it just happened by chance. I think all he really wants to do is make a beautiful dress, and there's nothing more difficult to do than make a beautiful dress.

But 60 years ago, the times were different. Ready-to-wear didn't really exist. Clothes that were made for you specially – that was the way people dressed. My mother, when she was a child in the '30s and '40s, always had her clothes made for her, whether it was by my grandmother or a local dressmaker. People didn't have ready-to-wear clothes. They bought a mixture of haute couture and dressmaker's clothes. There are so many stories from the time about women getting into huge trouble for having one dress made by Dior or Chanel and then having 25 copies made by their seamstress.

I don't think that necessarily happens nowadays. Haute couture itself has also changed enormously. But back then, the garments that sold were more discreet. Today, I do know that, from Dior's sales, the things that sell most of all are the things that are the most special. The things that are simpler, people don't want so much.

There's a certain level of fabric, technique, flattery and price that separates couture from ready-to-wear – but it's the eye of a great designer that is the most important. It has to have an element of fun. Imagine if you are spending £100K on an outfit; you'd want it to be fun. Within the world of haute couture, of course, there are some outfits that are made just for an image. But they're still made to sell.

What happens is a client will come in and see a crazy asymmetric thing with a giant bustle on it, and she'll say, "I'd like to have the same thing, but

"All the hats for Audrey Hepburn, all the hats from *Funny Face* were made in this workroom – and then I'm asking these people to make my hats!"

Left and below: Stephen Jones' millinery creations for his Autumn/Winter 2010 collection, called XYZ, including (top left) Triple Vision, (below left) Ultrasound, and (below right) Bang

Opposite, top: A Balenciaga sheath dress made in 1950. The skirt is decorated with individual pieces of chiffon attached to bands

Opposite, below right: Elsa Schiaparelli's famous shoe hat was conceived with Salvador Dalí and made in the winter of 1937-38 using black wool felt. There is one in The Metropolitan Museum of Art in New York

Opposite, below left: A late day dress by Jacques Fath, with a striped silk top, turned-back oversized lace cuffs and a full, tightly belted wool skirt. Photographed against Bernard Lamotte's French mural in 1949

"Haute couture was always about the pinnacle of design, combined with what the client wanted. Always, always, always"

smaller", or "I love the silhouette of that drapery, but it's too transparent, can I have it opaque?", or "I want that jacket, but I want it with a long skirt". This is the point. Haute couture was always about the pinnacle of design, combined with what the client wanted. Always, always, always.

I'm doing some research at the moment on Wallis Simpson. She would always work closely with the designers, because she had a fabulous collection of jewellery and she wanted the details of the clothes taken off so it wouldn't be too much with the jewellery. And designers like Balenciaga and Dior would always comply, because she was a great dresser. If you are a couturier, who are you to tell a client she is wrong? Of course, you have to maintain your level of taste, but your taste has to be mutable to fit in with that of your clients. To be a good couturier, you have to be a good talker, but you also have to be a good listener.

Couture will always evolve, and that's what keeps it relevant. For 2010, for example, they allowed all the big jewellers in Paris to be part of couture – as they should be. Maybe in 100 years' time it will be jewellers and shoemakers like Roger Vivier, and it will be a mixture of things. Pre-war haute couture was very different from post-war. And the only reason fashion can exist is because it marries well with its times. If it doesn't, it's an anachronism, and there's no point to it.

Biographical Notes

Stephen Jones was born in Cheshire in 1957. He studied fashion design at Central Saint Martins and frequented the New Romantic club Blitz. He began designing outlandish hats for himself and his friends – including Boy George, Duran Duran and Jean Paul Gaultier.

Jones designed a line of hats for Fiorucci in 1979 and, with financial backing from Blitz's owner, he opened his own millinery salon in Covent Garden the following year. His first Paris fashion show was in 1982; Princess Diana soon became a regular customer.

He has designed hats for the catwalk shows of Jean Paul Gaultier, Thierry Mugler, John Galliano at Dior, and Vivienne Westwood. His work is known for its inventiveness and high level of technical expertise. He gives names to most of his hat collections, such as The Hanging Gardens of Babylon (Spring/Summer 1981), Shriek with Chic (Spring/Summer 1991) and Murder by Millinery (Autumn/Winter 1997).

Jones co-curated the 2009 exhibition *Hats: An Anthology* at London's Victoria and Albert Museum; and a hat he designed for the cover of *Tatler* is now in the V&A collection.

The House of Chanel

As style icons go, Coco Chanel was the most famous woman of her time and the best possible advertisement for the chic, sophisticated, independent women of the day. During the '20s and '30s, her little black dresses, easy jersey fabrics, masculine tailoring and even trousers were matched by equally revolutionary bobbed haircuts and suntanned skin. Post-World War II, Chanel revived her couture house and asserted her style on the world once more. With couture, ready-to-wear, jewellery, watches, fragrance and more, Chanel became a global phenomenon. Twelve years after her death, Karl Lagerfeld reinvigorated the Chanel brand; today it is more than rightfully his. So very highly regarded by his peers, Lagerfeld has created an amalgam of Chanel's spirit and his own, making the house one of the fashion world's most famous names.

1883: Gabrielle Bonheur "Coco" Chanel is born one of six children, in Saumur, France on 19th August. From an early age she lived in poverty, but in later life she quietly "forgot" her origins.

1895: Chanel is sent to an orphanage run by nuns, where she is taught to sew. After a few years, she finds work in a dressmaker's. At weekends, she works at a tailor's shop frequented by young officers. It is here that she is thought to have met textile heir Étienne Balsan; she becomes his mistress.

1906: Chanel goes to live with Balsan at his country estate near Compiègne. Her association with him and his rich friends is beneficial to Chanel and, while mixing with this stylish set, she demonstrates her disdain for fripperies with a distinctively plain style. In terms of appearance, she rejects outright the social mores of the time.

1908: Chanel discovers a flair for hat design. She buys straw boaters from a nearby store and trims them herself with a considered amount of elegant ribbons and feathers. Chanel meets Arthur "Boy" Capel, a wealthy Englishman who later loans her his Paris apartment to start a hat business. After some considerable success, Capel advances her the money to rent a shop of her own.

> "Some people think luxury is the opposite of poverty. It is not. It is the opposite of vulgarity"
> **Coco Chanel**

1910: Chanel sets up a hat shop at 21 rue Cambon, Paris under the label Chanel Modes.

1913: Chanel opens a new boutique in Deauville. Her collection of hats expands to include simple, loose blouses and lightweight separates designed to be worn without corsets. Chanel was anticipating a growing popularity for the sort of practical yet elegant styles that she herself preferred. She gets her first mention in *Vogue*.

1914: The outbreak of the First World War introduces more practical thinking to women's attire, a move that suits Chanel's frill-free aesthetic.

1915: In spite of the war, the trade in luxury continues, and Chanel opens a new boutique in Biarritz. Her reputation grows, with *Harper's Bazaar* stating, "The woman who hasn't at least one Chanel is hopelessly out of the running in fashion."

1916: The staff of the combined Chanel stores totals 300.

A classic little black dress by Chanel, ca 1960

Coco Chanel with Lady Pamela Smith, 1932

Chanel adjusting a sleeve, 1961

1918: Chanel produces cardigans and twinsets, and adapts men's sweaters to be worn over straight skirts.

1919: Years later, Chanel would reveal that 1919 was the year she "woke up famous".

1920: Chanel introduces trousers for women, based on a sailor shape, which she calls "yachting pants". She uses her social life to advertise her aesthetic, and discovers that she can influence fashion on whim. Throughout the '20s, she introduces many ideas, including pea jackets, raincoats, short, thick wool coats, little black dresses and collarless tweed suits.

1921: Chanel launches its first fragrance, Chanel Nº 5.

1935: Chanel is at the height of her success. She employs more than 3,000 workers and owns five buildings in the rue Cambon.

1939: The couture house closes at the outbreak of war.

1954: The couture house reopens – Coco is now 71. Although initially the fashion world is shocked to see the reworked signature Chanel pre-war suits, by the '60s they have become a symbol of timeless luxury and elegance – especially when worn with a string of pearls and a quilted bag.

1955: Chanel creates the first of its iconic quilted leather handbags.

1971: Coco Chanel dies on 10th January. The House of Chanel is sold to the Wertheimer family.

1978: Under the ownership of Alain Wertheimer, a pret-a-porter line is launched.

1983: Karl Lagerfeld takes over as Chief Designer and changes Chanel's fashion aesthetic, adding the kind of humour and daring that Chanel would have appreciated. His debut show features a simple, full-length black silk gown with a high neck, long sleeves, a pearl rope belt and matching pearl earrings. They are modelled by Inès de la Fressange, who later joins the house as Lagerfeld's muse. The success that Lagerfeld brings to the company heralds the opening of more than 40 Chanel boutiques worldwide in the '80s.

1987: Lagerfeld reprises the LBD with a ruffle-necked crepe de Chine dress with a dropped waistline and flounced skirt. He wins France's Golden Thimble award for his Chanel haute couture collection.

1990s: Lagerfeld embraces the younger customer by teaming fishnets with bouclé suits, laced-up work boots with leather jackets and georgette skirts.

2010: Lagerfeld is awarded France's Légion d'honneur at the Elysée Palace, and Chanel is recognised as one of the most powerful brands in the fashion industry, with an estimated value of £8bn. The success of Lagerfeld's collections is put down to his careful referencing of the past without being too obviously nostalgic. He is known for his constant reinvention of the classic Chanel suit, which he treats with a certain amount of humour, keeping it constantly relevant for a new generation.

"For me, Chanel is like music. There are certain notes, and you have to make another tune with them"
Karl Lagerfeld

Lagerfeld's muse, Inès de la Fressange, 1986

Karl Lagerfeld at Chanel in 1983

Lagerfeld on the runway, 2010

I USED TO WORK WITH Mr de la Renta at Pierre Balmain in Paris. Being in a couture house was rather intimidating. The studio where all the garments were constructed was on the top floor in La Maison Balmain, and no one was allowed up there. You were not allowed to see the workers. They were kept completely in isolation. Except for the *première* – the person in charge – and she would come down with the garments to do the fittings, and then disappear back upstairs again.

I remember once when Mr de la Renta and I had done a fitting, half an hour later we said to each other, "Let's just take another look at that dress, one more time." And the première told me I couldn't see it. And I said, "Why not?" and she said, "It's gone." And I said, "What do you mean it's gone?" It kind of freaked me out, this approach. So I went upstairs to find it and when I got there, actually the entire dress had been dismantled. It really was gone. Disappeared. That is couture. You do a fitting with a dress and then you totally dismember it. Every single piece has to be adjusted to get the fit right. There are probably 10 ladies on one dress.

I hadn't done couture before. I didn't know. I thought if something doesn't fit, you do a pinch here and there and then, you know, it fits. But in couture it's different. That's why it's magic. If one little detail changes, then everything has to be corrected. Therein lies the difference. For me it was great to see this almost sacred secret space. After that incident, I sneaked up there all the time.

There are so many couturiers that have been inspirational over the last century. There are so many talents you can look at. Vionnet was so incredible, because she really mastered the bias cut. Her designs still look modern, even today. I could name other people as well who are just the opposite of Vionnet. I absolutely love Balenciaga, for example. I take great inspiration from him.

But Vionnet is just so current. I just love, love, love her work. When you encounter an original Vionnet piece, it is just so delicate and so smart. She was a master of cutting. She creates architecture with softness. She understood fabric. She understood how different fabrics behave. Good design comes from the immediacy of having the scissors and the fabric in your hand, instead of trying to understand a flat pattern. It's an emotional process. This is how I design. That's probably why I relate to her so much.

There are wonderful pictures of her pinning, draping and cutting fabric on her miniature forms. I believe that the testament of a good design is totally through the fabric. You have to understand what the fabric does, what its peculiarities and particularities are – how to translate a piece of fabric into a three-dimensional piece.

My favourite dress of Vionnet's was made up

Francisco Costa
Calvin Klein

"Good design comes from the immediacy of having the scissors and the fabric in your hand, instead of trying to understand a pattern. It's an emotional process. This is how I design"

of four square pieces of chiffon layered over each other – and they create a pattern. When you had the dress on, the fabric fell beautifully. The details are mirrored on two sides – the simplicity of it, the genius of it. You must remember that at that time designers like Paul Poiret were doing clothes that were so ornate they were almost like costumes. Everything was happening in Paris – the Ballets Russes brought so much glamour. And Vionnet was the antithesis of that aesthetic. Yet the quality of Vionnet's design spoke the loudest.

Balenciaga was a master. He had an incredible talent for shape and form. It's easy to see why he is so popular with so many designers; his creations are so glamorous and so bold, even today. He is chic, with his sense of colour and the severe, almost religious sensibilities of his work. There are so many Balenciaga garments that stay in one's mind. There was an incredible wedding dress that he did – the simplicity of the cut was perfect. He had a real love of organza. The nature of organza is that it gives more body to the silhouette. It was an incredible dress. The wedding cape was amazing – with a hat to match. When you see it, or a picture of it, you just go "wow". It's just so grand; it's just so beautiful. When I say grand I don't mean grand in the sense of showy – I mean the design was just so perfect.

There are so many people today trying to keep this magic going. I think Galliano does a fantastic job with it, and Lagerfeld is clever. Olivier Theyskens is doing some amazing things. Ghesquière is almost couture-like with his ready-to-wear, which is incredible. It's important to keep the skills involved in couture alive.

If I could have designed something, I guess it would have to be Dior's New Look – it was so iconic, obviously. But the New Look was about much more than just the garments. After all, they kind of existed already. I think Jacques Fath had done that shape long before Dior. It was all about the moment – all about timing. To introduce that reduction of waist and that explosion of skirt when he did, that's what made it special. I think the same is true of the Trapeze collection that Yves Saint Laurent introduced.

Of all the couture techniques, draping is the most magical. It's becoming less and less practised today. Letting the fabric dictate the design produces the best results. It's the opposite of manufacture. I remember Ungaro in the 1980s – he had an incredible passion and communication in his design. His draping was incredible. Watching him at work was amazing. Unfortunately, that art is disappearing.

As long as there's aspiration there will be a demand for clothes that are luxurious and relevant for a certain type of woman. We have become much more casual as a society in

terms of dress. But there are people who really understand couture, who really appreciate what it's about and want to be a part of it. Maybe there will be a shift in the way couture is done and how it is approached – but it is not the end of couture. Luxury is incredibly important: the luxury of time, the luxury of space, the luxury to appreciate.

Which of the couturiers would I like to have worked for? All of them! Of course Balenciaga. Vionnet also. If I had to choose… I suppose I am comfortable with Balenciaga; I understand him probably more than Vionnet. I understand how to make the Balenciaga aesthetic happen. So I would have to go with Vionnet.

There's a famous quote from Babe Paley when Balenciaga closed his doors. She said something like, "With Balenciaga gone, fashion is over." She was so upset. She mostly wore Balenciaga. But when you look through her wardrobe, she didn't buy fashion for fashion's sake; she was a collector of great style, made in a good way. So it wasn't just for show. These are clothes that will last. That's what separates couture from everything else. It's an understanding, an appreciation of handiwork. The perfection of imperfection. It's the imperfection that makes it perfect.

Biographical Notes

Calvin Klein was born in 1942 and studied at the Fashion Institute of Technology (FIT) before launching his eponymous label in 1968. Klein came to fame for creating the designer jean craze of the late 1970s – he sold 200,000 pairs in their first week – in part due to an advert featuring a 15-year-old Brooke Shields, with the slogan: "Nothing comes between me and my Calvins."

Francisco Costa was born in 1961 in Guarani, a small town in Brazil, where his mother had set up a childrenswear manufacturing business. After her death, Costa moved to New York in the early '90s without being able to speak a word of English. Like Calvin Klein, he studied at FIT. He then worked for Bill Blass, followed by Oscar de la Renta for five years – both on de la Renta's eponymous label – and at Balmain couture before joining Tom Ford at Gucci in 1998. Costa joined the Calvin Klein Group in 2001 and became Creative Director in 2003, hand-picked by Klein himself. While Costa has modernised the '90s austerity which earned the label the nickname "Calvin Clean", he has remained faithful to the minimalist aesthetic inherent to the house.

In 2006 and 2008, he won the coveted Council of Fashion Designers of America award for Womenswear Designer of the Year.

Right and below: Francisco Costa's Autumn/Winter 2010 collection for Calvin Klein was faithful to the label's iconic minimalism. Tailored trousers, cashmere coats with rounded shoulders, and silk shift dresses came in a mainly monochrome palette of black and white, with dashes of blue and silver. In a further nod to the '90s, Kirsty Hume, Stella Tennant and Kristen McMenamy all took to the catwalk

Opposite: A velvet sheath dress with fishtail skirt and tulle underskirts by Balenciaga. Photograph by Louise Dahl-Wolfe

"It is not the end of couture. Luxury is incredibly important: the luxury of time, the luxury of space, the luxury to appreciate"

Christian Lacroix

AS A CHILD GROWING UP IN ARLES, the nearest I got to proper haute couture was my mother's magazines. Ready-to-wear was available by then, but it was considered terribly cheap, and my parents were bourgeoisie – they had very good taste, but not necessarily the money to match.

During the '50s, there were probably around 30 seamstresses in Arles. They weren't couturiers by any means, but dressmakers who would get patterns from the haute couture houses and make up the styles of the day.

As a child, I was never very interested in needles, thread and the fabric of fashion, but I was fascinated by its incredible atmosphere of femininity. The dressmakers' workshops were a secret world of tulle, lace and complicated constructions.

I was born in 1951, so I must have been about two or three when the New Look was everywhere, although longer skirt lengths and volume remained popular for a few years after that. When my mother and her friends had coffee, I'd hide under the table, smell the fragrances and see the quality of their stockings and shoes. It was my first experience of fashion, my first touch of high-quality fabrics. Even then I noticed the difference between one fashion season and the next.

In Arles, at this time, for people like my parents, your fashion defined you. My mother told me she would rather stay at home than go out without wearing the right skirt at the right length. Later it was all about gingham because of Raquel Welch. Then it was suddenly dark grey denim worn with *broderie anglaise*, and all the ladies in Arles ripped apart their grandmothers' precious petticoats to trim their denim with lace. That was around 1956. Of course, none of this was proper couture. But later I did find a connection between Arles and real couture – Louis Féraud was born there. He made my mother's engagement suit and bridal gown, and went on to become a famous couturier. In the late '60s and early '70s, I was invited to his show, but by then couture was in a little bit of a decline – it had become flat.

In my twenties I was studying at the Sorbonne to become a museum curator, and thinking of sketching for maybe the theatre or stage. I hadn't thought about being a fashion designer. I was very bored there, because I'd been expecting something a little crazier, more arty – but it was full of very dull people. I wanted to tell my parents that I didn't want to do it any more, but I was too embarrassed. Anyway, at this time, I went to a dinner party and, as a thank you present, I sent a gift with a tiny sketch. The girl I sent it to was in fashion and she called me to say that my sketch reminded her of everything she had just seen at Paris Fashion Week. At that point I didn't even know what Fashion Week

"When my mother and her friends had coffee, I'd hide under the table, smell the fragrances and see the quality of their stockings and shoes"

was! That was 1978. She asked if I had any other sketches and sent me to see Madame Rooki, the director of Paris' best fashion school, who told me I was too old to start again at fashion school. Too old at 25! Besides, the school was quite expensive. But she thought I had something in the way I sketched and put colours together. She wrote some letters of recommendation, and I went to see a few people, such as Mr Lagerfeld. Finally, I got a job as an intern at Hermès and left the Sorbonne.

My first proper job was at Jean Patou. I had no formal training; everything I know about the history of costume I discovered for myself. My taste comes from within. My first collection was a nightmare, but the second had very good reviews. I had no experience, which, in hindsight, was probably quite a good thing. I noticed that the work of Claude Montana and Thierry Mugler – all the ready-to-wear runway at the time – had '40s couture effects – big hats and extravagance. So I thought, why not use haute couture ateliers to create a more coherent couture?

I've always been fascinated by old movies, especially musicals. I loved Poiret, Schiaparelli and Charles Worth. I love the history of costume, the theatre – Christian Bérard, the great fashion illustrator of the '40s, was always like, *wow* for me. Paris in the '40s has always fascinated me, and I've often wished I'd lived then – I was born just a few years too late. So with all these amazing references in my head, I developed the extravagant style for which I became known. Shocking pink, flowers, big hats, big prints and little prints. For many, many people it was awful, but others – especially Suzy Menkes and the *Herald Tribune's* Hebe Dorsey – supported me. For five years it was quite nice at Patou, but it was still ready-to-wear, and I was frustrated because everyone used to say, "It's so beautiful, but I can't afford it."

By chance I had dinner with someone who knew the head of Dior, and they said I should approach LVMH for backing. I had heard they were interested in me, but then nothing. So I just got on with my Patou collection. The night before my show, Hebe Dorsey called to say that I was going to need a very good lawyer to organise my contract at LVMH, and a few days later it was done. That was my path into couture.

I'm quite close to Azzedine Alaïa; his true God is Charles James. I didn't know much about James, but once I discovered his work I was amazed by the modernity of his designs. I don't think my style was inspired by Charles James because I'm not a cutter, but I am inspired by the quality of his work.

I'm most fascinated by the opposite of what I know how to do. The designers of the '50s, or those of the last century, are sketcher-designers.

There are some, like Azzedine or Balenciaga, who are out on their own. But now, after 30 years of fashion, I'm much more interested in the cut. Charles James' and Balenciaga's works are the opposite of mine; they are always refining and refining until they end up with the quintessence of the design.

I start the design process with sketching – the neck, breast, small of the back, the legs – then the rest comes. I totally agree with Dior when he said, "Couture is a marriage of design and material. There are instances of perfect harmony – and there are a few of disaster." You have to have a girl in mind when you design. If you don't, it's a nightmare. Of course, I am always opulent – I love extra everything – but I always start simply with the neck and the waist.

For me, ethnic things provide the most fascinating couture. No designer could ever have come up with what has evolved in culture. If you look at traditional costumes from middle Europe, the South of France, India or Spain, everything comes from the history of people – that is what I love. Nothing in haute couture can compete with original costumes. When I see something I like from, say, Galliano, it's because of its connection to another place and time. I always wish that I had a time machine so I could go back – not to see Cleopatra or Marie Antoinette or anything grand – just to see ordinary people, listen to their language and get a sense of the little details.

In the '70s, I especially loved Yves Saint Laurent's collections – the Rive Gauche line with all the prints and colours. If you dissect his sense of colour and how he designed, it's all connected to Schiaparelli, Balenciaga and Chanel. But I've always been fascinated by the 1940s, the drama and the violence of war just a few years before my birth. Each time you have such a crisis, fashion is in progress. During the First World War, Chanel started a trend for shorter skirts and shorter hair, while the reaction to the end of the Second World War in the late '40s was to bring back the romantic, nostalgic silhouettes of the turn of the century.

The fashion world today is so different. In the '60s, when Ossie Clark was designing, fashion was everywhere at the same time – on the catwalks, in magazines, in shop windows, on the street. People "followed" fashions. Nowadays there is a gap between what appears on the runways and what is worn on the street. And sometimes the street is just as interesting as the runway – especially in London.

But my way of designing – elaborate costumes with big skirts, big lace and everything – that is over. And young people today don't have the means to buy couture.

Opposite: A fancy-dress ensemble with turban by Paul Poiret from 1911. Poiret had been influenced by the costume designs of Léon Bakst for the Ballets Russes – as well as the art of ancient Greece – and introduced his jupe-culotte, or harem pants, in 1911. This 1002nd Night dress was made of silver lamé and green gauze and worn with harem pants. Paul Poiret's "style sultane" was a succès de scandale in France, with the designer accused of undermining Western values. He successfully sued for defamation

Left: Christian Bérard's drawing of a woman in a feather cape and purple chiffon gown by Jean Patou, from 1935. Bérard also illustrated for Coco Chanel, Nina Ricci and Elsa Schiaparelli

It's also sad to see what the fashion press used to be and what it is today. Now it is totally cold, totally ruled by money. There is nothing daring any more. Of course, I miss couture. But it's like any surgery – you have a leg cut off and eventually you get used to it.

But now I'm enjoying designing for the theatre. I had an opening at the Berlin Opera House last year for an opera by Handel. The director asked me to create some contemporary costumes, and some people in the audience asked me if the costumes were available to buy. So I thought, why not sell the costumes? In a really big opera, you have a very beautiful workroom with a team of very good seamstresses. So I'm designing more and more for the stage now and, for me, it feels very much the same as couture.

> "Of course, I miss couture. But it's like any surgery – you have a leg cut off and eventually you get used to it"

Biographical Notes

Christian Lacroix was born in 1951 in Arles, in the South of France. He studied art history at the University of Montpellier, and museum studies at the Sorbonne.

After working as a fashion assistant at Hermès, he designed accessories at Guy Paulin, then went to an haute couture firm in Tokyo for a year before becoming Head Designer at Jean Patou from 1981 to 1986.

In 1987 he launched his own couture house in Paris, backed by LVMH. His collections have been likened to "an extravagant Technicolor musical from the golden age of Hollywood".

He sent shock waves through the fashion world with his eclectic approach to fabrication and elaborate, often costume-inspired designs. Dramatic taffeta gowns, baroque details and searing clashing colours and patterns are all signatures of Lacroix.

The house was closed in 2009, and Lacroix now spends his time designing for the theatre and curating exhibitions. His fans, however, remain loyal.

Opposite: From Christian Lacroix's Autumn/Winter 2009 haute couture show (top left, bottom right), his final runway show; and (top right, bottom left) from his Autumn/Winter 2008 collection

Right: An evening dress by Elsa Schiaparelli from Autumn/Winter 1950, a collection she called The Front Line

Below: A Charles James Balloon dress from 1955. James was known for eschewing trends, and instead drawing on references from the past, in particular from French historical costumes and neoclassical paintings by Ingres

Bottom: Fashion illustrator René Gruau's drawing of one of Christian Dior's iconic New Look dresses from 1947

MY FIRST EXPERIENCE OF COUTURE? I remember precisely; I was 12. I was in Cannes during the film festival. It was the holidays from school. We were staying in Luberon, in Aix-en-Provence, and we went down to the coast for two days. It was in the '70s and we knew the festival was on and we wanted to have a look – see what it was all about.

There was just a small palace at the festival at the time – a tiny place with steps, like a sort of house. We saw a lot of people. We thought there must be something happening. So we went closer. Suddenly we saw a woman with a blonde chignon. She was wearing a long dress – and it was really weird because it was during the day and she seemed overdressed. And I thought she must be an actress. It was the first time I had ever seen anyone who might be famous.

There were many photographers around her. And the girl with her white dress and her navy shawl and her chignon, she walked really slowly forwards and then she turned and, as she walked back, she looked directly at the cameras, dropped the shawl a little and posed.

I had never seen anyone posing before in my life. Up until that point I had thought that women in magazines stood that way naturally. I hadn't known it was a job, that it was her job to do that. That there was a lot of work involved in these pictures in magazines. It was Grace Kelly. It was a real couture moment. A real Hollywood moment. And when she turned back again, everyone knew that the moment was over. And the photographers knew to put their cameras away. Not like today.

The dress was draped from the shoulder with maybe three pleats, and there was a really large belt in navy. It was Givenchy, I think. In the '70s and early '80s, Givenchy was very navy and white – without it looking nautical. It was very beautiful.

I did know Yves Saint Laurent, although I wasn't a close friend. He has got to be considered the most inventive designer because he worked for maybe 40 years – more than any other designer. Madame Chanel lasted 20 years, from 1919 to 1939 – though it's true she opened again in 1954. Christian Dior was only famous from 1947 to 1957. Yves Saint Laurent has the record for longevity and is, I think, by far the most inspirational couturier ever.

I worked with the brand YSL a lot during the '80s. But my relationship with Yves Saint Laurent the couturier began properly when I heard that he was doing his final show. I had designed a shoe that I didn't want to be ready-to-wear because I thought it was a very symbolic shoe. So I kept it. And when I heard about his last show, I was in Italy and I did the first prototype. It was a very simple shoe – it had just the YSL logo, pavéed in

Christian Louboutin

diamonds on the front and nothing else. It was almost like a tattoo of diamonds. I sent the shoe to Yves and Loulou de la Falaise, his muse; he loved it, and said he would like to have it for the last look at the very end of the show. For me that was fantastic. I was very proud.

Many of Yves Saint Laurent's shows stick in my mind. There were so many outfits that were incredible. The one that comes immediately to mind is a dress he did with the French sculptor François-Xavier Lalanne. It had a bustier in gold metal. This part up here in gold represented the breasts and then below it was all fluffy chiffon – navy or black. Irving Penn took a lot of pictures – in black and white – so it looks black. Yves Saint Laurent was the master at working in chiffon. The dresses always had incredible construction, and yet it looked as though he had put two pins into a piece of fabric and there it was – flying. But I looked inside the dresses and, you know, they had a very specific construction.

Azzedine Alaïa never claimed to be a couturier. He doesn't show in the couture calendar but, for me, he is definitely the most inspirational modern couturier. I saw Alaïa working many times and he just knows; fashion comes naturally to him. The reason I think I understand Alaïa so well is that we have one very important thing in common. We both really like the feminine form. Before I met Alaïa, I remember seeing some pictures of him working on the Crazy Horse Girls in the late '70s. He is completely overwhelmed by the feminine shape – obsessed, in a nice way, by the female form. This makes him completely different.

Because he designs on real people, he has a great sense of how the fabric will work – whether it is silk, leather or whatever – how the textiles will wrap around the figure. He doesn't have an idealised view of the female body; he doesn't think of women as photographs who have to be skinny. He respects their natural figure. He never works on sticks – I am with him on that.

Over the past decade, there has been such easy access to luxury that it has lost something. Now there is a category of people who want less easy access to something that is more special. I hope this will give new life to couture. Couture has changed. Couture is now in the hands of a very few people. But the people who want couture now are also different. And the way that everyone is living is different.

Those huge dresses in the couture shows – I find them very beautiful. Some of my friends who are clients of couture look at those dresses and would be happy to borrow one. But the obvious question is not only where do you go in that dress, but how do you get there…in a carriage? No matter what your wealth, the modern life doesn't suit taking a ball gown

around with you – even if you have your own plane. So those dresses which are spectacular and beautiful, to me those are showpieces, but not couture. Couture used to exist to fit in with the lives of clients. Back then, if you had an important lunch, then you had your dress tailored to look good at the lunch. Now if you have an important lunch, you are not going to go for couture. Couture has been pushed to a place that is no longer relevant to people's lives. There is a detachment.

That's why I think that Azzedine is one of the few remaining true couturiers: when he designs, before he starts, he thinks to himself, my woman is going to be on a plane; she doesn't want to have to wait for her suitcase; she wants to travel light; she wants to leave in a second. So the suit she's in needs to be comfortable, to give freedom. A lot of women work now – they are not just standing around posing in their dresses. So couture had to change. There are more demands on your clothes. And even if you have bought these amazing dresses, unless you receive at home, how do you even get in a car?

Couture is a parade – it's a super-interesting laboratory of ideas – but it's away from where it was. It allows designers to try different techniques. It's great that it exists. It's very interesting. Couture has become incredibly interesting, but less liveable in.

Biographical Notes

Christian Louboutin was born in 1964 in Paris. He is known worldwide for his red sole design, which was created when he put red nail polish on the sole of one of his designs; it soon became a permanent fixture. For a short period, he designed shoes with baby blue soles, as "something blue" for his bridal clients.

His career in fashion began at age 17, when he got a job as an apprentice in the dressing rooms of the Folies Bergère music hall in Paris.

From there he went to Charles Jourdan and did freelance designs for Chanel and Yves Saint Laurent. He launched his own label and opened his first boutique in 1991. He helped bring stilettos back into fashion in the '90s and 2000s, designing dozens of styles with five-inch heels and higher.

He has collaborated with the biggest brands in fashion, including Roland Mouret, Chloé, Lanvin, Alexander McQueen and Viktor & Rolf.

The Luxury Institute's Luxury Brand Status Index declared his shoes the Most Prestigious Women's Shoes in 2007, 2008 and 2009. Celebrities who wear his designs include Kate Moss, Nicole Kidman and Madonna.

Top: Princess
Grace of Monaco
captured amidst
the crowds on the
Croisette in Cannes
during the film
festival in the 1970s

Above: From Yves
Saint Laurent's
final show in 2002,
closing with a model
in a Le Smoking suit
wearing Louboutin's
shoes with "YSL"
pavéed in diamonds

Left: A drawing by
Thierry Perez of a
long black chiffon
dress specially
created by Azzedine
Alaïa in 1987 for
Naomi Campbell
as an homage to
both Madeleine
Vionnet and
Josephine Baker

Opposite: Shoes
from Christian
Louboutin's
Autumn/Winter 2010
collection – all with
the signature
red soles

Hannah Marshall

I'M A BIG FAN OF THE SHOULDER PAD. Some might say I'm slightly obsessed with the shoulder pad. I blame Balenciaga. But Cristóbal is very relevant right now, so I would have to say that from my "personal history of couture" point of view, Cristóbal is a great inspiration.

It's hard to pinpoint just one couturier, though, who I would say is the *most* inspirational. There are so many. Coco Chanel, obviously, is a major one for me – but it's also incredible how Karl Lagerfeld has brought the fashion house into the 21st century and made it really contemporary; that is a real inspiration. He has somehow kept the essence of Chanel – the ethos that the house stood for – but made it modern so that people can connect to it. It feels so current. You have really cool people like Alexa Chung who have really connected to the brand – that's an incredible achievement when you consider that the house is 100 years old.

I used to read about haute couture in magazines and books when I was a child, and it seemed so very untouchable. It was like a dream world. When I was doing my degree, I learned more about the art of tailoring. We had an amazing tutor who had examples of couture jackets, and he showed us what went on on the insides, and the sorts of techniques you need to know to be able to create a perfectly tailored jacket. We learned how to do hand canvassing and everything that goes into shaping. It's not just about sculpting a garment; it's about transforming the natural silhouette.

The technique that I find most amazing is to do with this construction. It's very relevant to my aesthetic. My work is all about creating sculpture around the body – using clean lines and a stripped-away silhouette. Most of the work that goes into my designs happens between the outside fabric and the lining. The fusings, the paddings – these are employed in the highly skilled techniques that really seem to belong to another time.

I studied art and design – but the degree I studied was really broad, so I was able to cross over into different disciplines that were outside of fashion design. Quite often I would find myself working in a 3D workshop with metal, or in a photographic studio taking pictures of my designs. I really loved the fact that I was free to be creative.

I've got a huge collection of fashion books full of Post-it notes. One of the first books I bought included an amazing image of a Schiaparelli dress that I really love. It's a really beautiful black dress, of course, with padding and embroideries all over it that depict a kind of exoskeleton. It's the simplicity of the cut, the beautiful fabric and the interesting way it's three-dimensional.

"My work is all about creating sculpture around the body – using clean lines and a stripped-away silhouette"

This is a really specialist technique where you get two layers of fabric: the bottom one is very sheer, and you stitch a pattern to join them together, then pierce the back and fill it with thread. I can't remember what it's called. But that technique and that Schiaparelli dress inspired my last collection. It was all about surveillance society and ways of protecting the body – and having the inside on the outside, and different spine details in different areas. Jessica Alba wore one of my dresses a couple of weeks ago. It's called the Spineback dress. It's black leather. It has three-dimensional details that come right out of the back. It took so long to produce.

We did a one-sleeve version that Janet Jackson wore on the cover of *Wonderland*. I want to do a few pieces in each collection that are almost crafted. I spent so many hours on it. I guess it's a bit like couture.

As a designer, it's nice to not worry about how I'm going to sell this, or who is going to buy that, and almost take all those aspects away and just create really beautiful pieces. They might take 10 hours or 50 hours or hundreds of hours to produce but, when the cost isn't an issue, that doesn't matter.

So there are some pieces in the collection where I try not to think about the commercial side. With most of the collection, it's important to be careful about money – but there are showpieces where you forget about that and try to really get across what you are thinking about for that season.

If I could work for one couturier, it would have to be Thierry Mugler, when he was doing incredible pieces in the '80s. He's been such an inspiration to me. Still, every season, there's something in my mind that he created. He really knew how to play around with the silhouette – to create a second skin with an armour-like quality. I have collected so many pictures of his designs on my computer – sculptural, leather, black and exquisitely made.

Mugler was one of the first designers I was introduced to when I started my degree. There was another girl on the course who I got friendly with. She was in her final year. She loaned me this Mugler book and I never gave it back – it was so amazing. I get inspiration from anywhere – from everything around me – from our voyeuristic society or art or music. I wouldn't say that I take direct references from couture, but you will always find something, a technique or a silhouette, in each collection.

I suppose it's apt that I should be inspired by Schiaparelli since she was one of the first designers to champion the shoulder pad. She was also not afraid to be different. She invented 12 commandments for women, one of which

Left: A Balenciaga dress photographed by George Hoyningen-Huene for Harper's Bazaar, December 1939

Below: Thierry Mugler's 1990s rubber-tyre suit. Mugler created the costumes for Beyoncé's I Am Sasha Fierce tour

Bottom: Schiaparelli worked with Salvador Dalí to create her silk crepe Skeleton dress (1938). Her clients included Mae West, whose torso inspired the bottle for her 1937 perfume, Shocking

Opposite: From Hannah Marshall's Autumn/ Winter 2010 Army of Me collection, with its exaggerated shoulders and revealing slits inspired by Grace Jones and art director Jean-Paul Goude

said: "Ninety percent of women are afraid of being conspicuous and of what people will say. So they buy a grey suit. They should dare to be different." I am right behind that.

In a way, I think couture should be a little bit mad. It should be exciting, for special occasions. It should be fun.

Couture clients are so lucky to be involved in such a special process – to be able to work so closely with a designer is, I imagine, an amazing collaborative experience. The amount of time it takes and the amount of love and care that goes into it – you want to be able to enjoy it.

> "I love Schiaparelli's dress... that depicts a kind of exoskeleton. It's the simplicity of the cut, the beautiful fabric and the interesting way it's three-dimensional"

Biographical Notes

Brought up in Colchester in Essex, Hannah Marshall studied fashion at the Colchester School of Art and Design, graduating with a first-class degree in fashion in 2003. She works from her studio in East London. Marshall began working as an intern for Jonathan Saunders in 2005 and set up her own label in 2007. Her first two collections were exhibited at OnOff and her third was shown as part of the British Fashion Council's New Generation initiative with three consecutive seasons of sponsorship

Marshall designs almost exclusively in black, and has been credited with reinventing the little black dress with her signature tough-luxe aesthetic. Her body-conscious dresses, with exaggerated silhouettes, often feature messages in Braille; her first collection featured velvet with laser-cut Braille words.

British supermodel Erin O'Connor loaned Marshall's iconic trapeze dress to the Little Black Dress exhibition at Zandra Rhodes' Fashion and Textile Museum in London.

Marshall has designed for Janet Jackson, Marina and the Diamonds, Skin of Skunk Anansie, Alison Mosshart of The Kills and Florence Welch of Florence and the Machine. Marshall had her first on-schedule show in February 2010, showing her Autumn/Winter 2010 collection, Army of Me. In March 2010, Marshall was invited to a Buckingham Palace reception in celebration and support of the British clothing industry.

The House of Lanvin

Jeanne Lanvin's original designs have often been captured in sophisticated 1920s illustrations that serve to imbue them with the romantic quality they deserve. Lanvin was something of an anomaly. While Chanel, Lelong and Patou were seen as modernists ridding the female form of constricting corsetry and promoting a more practical approach, Lanvin used the history of costume and the wide-ranging decorative arts to create her own modern signature style. Her gentle ideal of femininity has been reworked for the 21st century in the accomplished hands of Alber Elbaz, making Lanvin one of the most sought-after fashion brands in the world.

1867: Jeanne Lanvin is in born in Brittany, in northern France.

1883: Lanvin becomes an apprentice in a milliner's in Rue du Faubourg Saint-Honoré.

1885: With the financial assistance of a client, Lanvin sets up a workshop.

1889: The launch of the Lanvin label takes place at 16 rue Boissy-d'Anglas. She specialises in hats. She also designs a wardrobe for her daughter, which draws attention from customers.

1908: A children's department opens, and Lanvin begins to create matching mother-daughter garments. The Lanvin logo – of a mother and daughter – reflects her speciality.

1909: With a children's and womenswear department, Lanvin is allowed to join France's Chambre Syndicale de la Haute Couture.

"Modern clothes need a certain romantic feel"
Jeanne Lanvin

1910: Thanks to the popularity of Diaghilev's Ballets Russes, a new trend for Orientalism becomes a major influence on Lanvin, and her signature embroidery begins to be featured.

1913: Lanvin develops her "robes de style" look. Based on 18th-century designs, the full-skirted dresses become something of a trademark and continue to be popular until the early '20s.

1920: Lanvin's creative range allows her to expand her empire into an interiors range, known as Lanvin Décoration. This is followed by sportswear, perfume and lingerie lines.

1923: Lanvin expands her horizons once again with the opening of a dye factory in Nanterre where she can create her own specific shades, as well as a perfume laboratory.

1924: The first stores are opened outside Paris, in Cannes and Le Touquet, in northern France. Barcelona and Buenos Aires also gain stores.

1926: Lanvin receives the Chevalier de la Légion d'honneur in recognition of her work.

Fashion illustrations for Lanvin, 1925

Lanvin's "robes de style" in silk organdie, 1925

Jeanne Lanvin fits a model in Paris in the 1920s

1927: Arpège, Lanvin's signature fragrance, is released.

1938: At 71, Lanvin receives her second award. This time, she is named Officier de la Légion d'honneur.

1946: Lanvin dies at the age of 79. Her daughter Marie-Blanche de Polignac becomes the Director General.

1950: Antonio Canovas del Castillo del Rey, who previously worked for Elizabeth Arden in New York, becomes Lanvin's designer, and the house is known as Castillo for Lanvin. Castillo's first collection includes mink-trimmed white satin evening gowns that follow the design of the original "robes de style". He stays until 1963.

1964: Jules-François Crahay, formerly of Nina Ricci, begins designing Lanvin's couture collections. Known for a folk sensibility, he stays with the brand for 20 years.

1990: Claude Montana joins Lanvin for a short period, designing seven collections. He gives the brand a clean, minimal look and wins two Dé d'Or awards.

1993: The House of Lanvin withdraws from haute couture.

A dress by Castillo for Lanvin, 1956

1998: After Dominique Morlotti leaves the brand, Cristina Ortiz (who previously worked at Prada) heads up women's ready-to-wear.

2001: Alber Elbaz is appointed Creative Director of Lanvin. Originally from Casablanca, he previously designed for Geoffrey Beene, Guy Laroche and Yves Saint Laurent.

2002: Elbaz shows his first ready-to-wear collection for Lanvin. His modern take on French couture is established, characterised by raw hems, draping and sumptuous satins.

2005: Lanvin begins to gain a celebrity clientele, with Nicole Kidman and Chloë Sevigny wearing the brand's clothes on the red carpet.

2006: Elbaz brings back the signature "Lanvin blue", and it is used for all of the brand's packaging.

2007: Elbaz is named one of *Time* magazine's 100 Most Influential People in the World. The same year, he follows in Jeanne Lanvin's footsteps and receives the Chevalier de la Légion d'honneur.

Jules-François Crahay designs for Lanvin, 1974

2009: Lanvin has a turnover of £140m and sells in approximately 450 stores.

2009: Lanvin collaborates with Swedish jeans brand Acne to create a limited-edition range.

2010: Elbaz continues to create new pieces honouring Jeanne Lanvin's legacy. The brand's Autumn/Winter collection features embroidery and full-skirted dresses.

"There is nothing scarier than being 'the designer of the moment', because the moment ends. When I was hired at Lanvin, it dawned on me that the one thing I had to do there was go back to basics. The challenge now is to make everything about design rather than style"
Alber Elbaz

Alber Elbaz on the runway, 2010

Gilles Mendel
J. Mendel

I HAVE BEEN INTERESTED IN FASHION for as long as I can remember. My mother was a little diva. She used to be with designers all the time – from Jean-Charles de Castelbajac to Azzedine Alaïa. She had an incredible appetite for fashion; I think I lived fashion through her from a very young age. But I guess I got serious about fashion when I came to New York in the early '80s.

My school of fashion was learning at the atelier of my father, J. Mendel, where I met people with incredible craftsmanship. My father and my grandfather were highly skilled artisans working with fur. It was there that I learned the value of construction – that a successful piece of clothing was an equal balance of construction and style.

One of the most inspirational haute couture designers is Madame Vionnet. She is someone I have loved for many years. I have always been entranced by the construction of her gowns. There is a language in Madame Vionnet's designs that has very much to do with what I try to do today. Her collections were always very light and airy. She was one of the first designers to make clothes with transparency that also had some kind of construction behind them. She was amazing for her time, one of the most extraordinary designers of the 20th century.

The very first season I did ready-to-wear, I was asked to make a dress for Laura Linney, for the Oscars. It was my very first couture gown. It was very exciting to have something on the red carpet. We used embroidery on organza so that it looked like feathers, which was done by Lemarié, one of the couture ateliers in Paris. It transformed the hard fabrication of gazar into something light and incredibly delicate. They also make the most beautiful flowers for Chanel in Paris. That was my first couture moment in New York.

One of the more recent couture designers who continues to inspire me is Christian Lacroix. He has an extraordinary ability to combine all colours and all prints together at the same time in one piece of clothing. He has a very contemporary approach.

The one piece of clothing that I would have loved to have designed is a piece from Madame Grès. Why? Because at the very beginning, when I started designing couture and ready-to-wear clothing, I was inspired by her pleating. If you look at my label's DNA today, you will see that we rediscovered some of the hand-pleating techniques that you see in Madame Grès' designs. A lot of the dresses in my collections feature this hand-pleating technique, which is done in my atelier here in New York. It is very labour-intensive; it requires precision and highly skilled hands, and it is very hard to replicate. I suppose that's why not many people do it now. Technology can never replace the handwork

of couture. It is impossible. Recently I designed some theatre costumes, and for speed, and to save money, we tried to reproduce the hand-pleating that I do in my own atelier on a machine. And even that did not work. There's a touch when it's done by hand that cannot be replicated – a machine is too regular. It can repeat the same thing indefinitely. Couture has always been unique, something that you cannot duplicate. You can feel the hand in couture. That's what makes it couture.

Couture can sometimes have a very old feeling – like a vintage look – to it. What Madame Grès did was take it into a modern arena. She used techniques that we associate with classical design and made very modern and young pieces. She didn't just make Greek-goddess-style dresses; she also created very revealing cuts for the time. There are photographs of models in her designs on the beach with their backs showing. That was groundbreaking. But the technique, the couture of the clothes, was impeccable.

That's why I find Lacroix so interesting. He has moved couture to another level. It's not couture as costume; it's not couture looking back to a time when ladies were corseted. There is no stiffness. The modernity in the way he worked the clothes is an expression of our time.

In times when the economy is not great and when people are far more conscious of spending money – in this world of thoroughly disposable clothes – couture has even more sense to exist. Couture has a real value. It is something unique. There is a consumer out there who wants to buy quality, like a piece of art, with historic value that will last for generations. There is a vast distance between affordable, disposable clothes and couture – but they coexist, and there is the wealth out there to afford true quality.

I have seen in books the beautiful ateliers of the '30s through to the '60s – this is when the ateliers were extraordinary with "hands". The role of the designer in those times was that of a conductor with an orchestra of virtuosos who were all highly skilled masters of their respective crafts and who had a real passion for what they did. When you look back at Balenciaga, for example, he was surrounded by the most incredible team, and they had licence to be extremely innovative. He is a perfect example of the best kind of couturier. Like Christian Dior and Yves Saint Laurent, he really invented new proportions with every new collection. In the '40s and '50s, each collection was a completely new fashion. In those days, there were a huge number of skilled hands employed. But today this is difficult to continue. There are fewer couture houses in the world and, because of that, there are fewer people trained in the art of couture

"I think couture should be a dream beyond the realities of the real world. It is pure creativity. It's an art form. It has to bring fantasy"

skills. I don't think those skills will necessarily die out, but they will become more precious and more rare. There will always be people who value couture and create a demand.

I think couture should be a dream beyond the realities of the real world. It is pure creativity. It's an art form. It has to bring fantasy.

Ultimately, the sort of couture that we are talking about is too expensive to produce. People don't want to do it because it is too time-consuming and labour-intensive. Mine is one of the last couture houses in New York. To get the level of detail that I require means that you have to have your own atelier. That's what it all comes back to. You have to control your own level of love. Couture is all about love.

If someone asked me to do couture for a big French fashion house, I would love to. It is a dream. I would be there in a moment. Meanwhile, I don't mind if people want to come to me in New York, to my atelier, for my couture.

> "You have to have your own atelier. That's what it all comes back to. You have to control your own level of love. Couture is all about love"

Biographical Notes

J. Mendel started life as a furrier in Paris in 1870, creating sophisticated fur pieces for the Russian aristocracy. The house is now located in New York, with the fifth-generation Gilles Mendel at the helm.

Mendel began his career apprenticing under his father, Jacques, at the J. Mendel Paris fur salon. In 1985, the label relocated to New York.

Mendel is known for showing fur's versatility and unexpected lightness, particularly in his ready-to-wear collection, launched in 2003.

Mendel is best known for his pleated silk chiffon evening gowns, which are made in his New York atelier. He was admitted into the Council of Fashion Designers of America in 2003 and presented his first ready-to-wear catwalk show at New York Fashion Week in 2004.

Clients include Kate Hudson, Diana Kruger and Kristen Stewart, who wore a cream J. Mendel dress at the November 2009 Rome photo call of *The Twilight Saga: New Moon*. His Resort 2011 collection was inspired by the costumes he designed for the New York City Ballet's production of *Call Me Ben*.

Above: A floor-length evening gown from the atelier of Madeleine Vionnet photographed by Horst for Vogue in 1935. The gown is draped to accentuate the silhouette, emphasising the free movement of the body. It suggests a dancer's fluidity by drawing on the classical influences that had an impact on Vionnet's designs

Right: An asymmetric evening gown by Madame Grès made in 1930 and still popular in the mid-1950s, when this photograph was taken for Vogue. A trained sculptor, Grès specialised, like Vionnet, in draping and hand-pleating techniques inspired by the cloaks, chiton and peplos of Greek antiquity. Grès' clients included Marlene Dietrich, Jackie Onassis and Barbra Streisand

Opposite: From J. Mendel's Autumn/ Winter collection, shown in New York in February 2010, featuring strapless, hand-pleated red-carpet eveningwear in slate blue organza and dark green silk mousseline

GLAMOUR WAS EVERYWHERE when I was growing up. The '60s were a special moment for fashion. My favourite television programme as a child was *Bewitched*. I loved the way the mother, Endora, was always so overdressed – she was very couture. In the old movies – the "real" movies that were on television during the '60s – all the leading ladies were dressed in couture. There's *The Women* by George Cukor – it was made in 1939 and has all the great stars of the day, including Joan Crawford, Rosalind Russell and Norma Shearer. And I was inspired from the youngest age by the image of Jackie Kennedy. And then Bianca Jagger. And the dresses of Halston.

And this was all on top of the imagery I was getting from growing up in the Missoni family. I don't have any experience of couture ateliers or workshops, but I remember every single thing about the history of Missoni. I was right there. They did a show in 1965 in a theatre in Milan – the first show – and I was there. They had a white screen on the stage, with the girls silhouetted behind it getting changed. It was absolutely outrageous – a game of shadows. And at the end of the show, the screen disappeared and all the girls came out. It was totally new and unexpected for 1965. But for me it was just my family, my life – I took it all for granted. The second show was in a swimming pool in Milan, and they had girls and boys floating on inflatable furniture – this was 1967 or '68 – even now that would be considered avant-garde.

Fashion has always been part of my life and holds no fear for me. When my mother asked me to take over designing the main line – up until that point I was developing research in knitwear and little by little adding to the collection – I was surprised. I was the third child. I think that was lucky for me. All the expectation had been lived out through the careers of my older siblings. I have always been free to express myself. I was quite shy through my teenage years. And I did not express myself at all creatively. So when my mother noticed that I could design, I think she was taken aback. She didn't know I knew how to put together a collection. She said, "Have you ever thought about designing the main line? Because what you are doing is what I would like Missoni to look like." I think she was feeling her age – she felt fashion is a younger person's game. She was trapped in a zigzag cage.

When I took over, I went ahead and designed what I liked. Commerciality can get in the way of fashion. The financial department tells you what sold well last season and they want some more of the same – it all gets too commercial. They don't like to let you go ahead and change. But today luxury is all about uniqueness. Missoni started producing outfits in limited numbered editions some years ago. Everyone now wants exclusivity and limited editions – personalised, customised garments are constantly requested.

The most extreme form of fashion is now couture. I believe that a dress must always be wearable – unwearable clothes are sculptures, works of art, images to look at. But haute couture should also be about a sense of fun and adventure. If there is no humour, no eccentricity, no will of transgression, then fashion becomes too functional. Inspirational and elegant couture will never be created by perceived "good taste".

For Missoni, Coco Chanel has to be the most important designer in history, because she changed the way women thought about clothes. It wasn't just about the unstructured silhouette and lack of corsetry – it was the very idea of using certain materials in a different way. She made it acceptable to use knitted fabrics and stretch fabrics for daywear. She started using jersey as a regular fabric, as well as wovens. That is how my mother started the Missoni approach. We are a knitwear company, but an unusual one, because we do fully fashioned garments that are knitted to fit the shape of the body, and we also do "cut and sew", where we treat knitted fabrics in the same way as a woven.

When I design, I don't get particularly inspired by couture, because we work with very clean shapes. There's nothing Baroque about Missoni. However, there are some crucial designs from the past that I always find instructive. Vionnet's "minimal" constructions, where she demonstrated her ability with the bias cut – I find that level of craftsmanship very inspirational.

Couture is well known for hiding the construction – I love invisible solutions. And when you see a couture dress that is so constructed that it virtually stands on its own – that's what I admire about couture. When worn, it redesigns the body, making it look beautiful, seductive and well dressed. We need to keep this craftsmanship alive. Couture should be the most refined fashion of its time, the purest form of research – this way we may be able to preserve and develop the know-how that could otherwise vanish.

The Chanel suit is, of course, the most timeless garment in history, and the Yves Saint Laurent tuxedo will never fall from style. Chanel continues to inspire me with her never-ending essentiality, purity and freshness. And you cannot mention couture without admiring Balenciaga's work. His understanding of the peculiarities of fabric, the way it could hold a shape, led his garments to become wearable sculpture.

The world of couture today is enhanced by Karl Lagerfeld, who I first met in the 1970s when he started working for Fendi. It is incredible what Karl has done at Chanel and the longevity of

> "If there is no humour, no eccentricity, no will of transgression, then fashion becomes too functional. Inspirational and elegant couture will never be created by perceived 'good taste'"

Left: Two models wearing Madeleine Vionnet's sleeveless evening gowns (1930): a black V-neck velvet dress with a white ermine band trimmed around the skirt hem and a white crepe V-neck dress with panne velvet bias-cut skirt

Below: An early photograph of Coco Chanel in the 1920s – the hedonistic era of flappers – wearing a silk satin coat trimmed in fur and her signature pearls

Opposite: From Missoni's Autumn/Winter 2010 collection, which included capes, kilts and coats held together with oversized safety pins and zips. Different fabrics and prints – including variations of the signature Missoni zigzag knit – were patchworked together

"A dress must always be wearable – unwearable clothes are sculptures, works of art... Couture should be about a sense of fun and adventure"

collaboration between them. What makes Karl a truly great designer is his ability to work for the fashion house. You can find young designers who have an incredible vision within their own companies, but when they join an established fashion house that already has an image, they must learn to work with, understand and respect that identity. This is what Karl has done at Chanel and, indeed, at Fendi.

Today it is vital for any fashion house to have a distinctive identity – to be recognised for a signature. To do nice clothes is too easy. In every fashion collection, you can find nice clothes – something you might like to wear. But without a clear brand identity, the house has no personality. I think Missoni has proved this; my parents invented fashion personality.

Biographical Notes

Missoni is based in Varese, Italy, and is most famous for its unique knitwear made from a variety of colourful, zigzagged or striped patterns. Angela Missoni's parents, Ottavio and Rosita, founded the label in 1953, the year they were married. They met at the 1948 Olympic games in London. In 1967, Rosita made headlines by instructing her models to go bra-less at a fashion show in Florence.

Angela took over designing in 1997. Her brother Vittorio is now the company chairman, while her daughter Margherita, is the brand's Ambassador and designed the accessories for the Autumn/ Winter 2010 show. Angela's most successful campaign was with Kate Moss as Brigitte Bardot for Autumn/Winter 2004. Angela is known for putting a modern spin on the traditional Missoni style to appeal to younger audiences. In 2009, Angela won the World Fashion Award.

Missoni opened the first of a planned series of lifestyle hotels in Edinburgh in 2009. Celebrities such as Sandra Bullock, Eva Mendes and Cate Blanchett have all worn Angela's designs. Missoni designs have been showcased at London's Victoria and Albert Museum.

THERE IS NOT ONE COUTURIER that I would say is more important than another. If I had to choose, I would go for Coco Chanel. I admire her for the story behind her. You can't help but love the histories of other people. You hear about them in books, or on the TV. It is amazing how someone can come from a really poor background and take all the references of their life and introduce them into clothes.

She had an understanding of what she wanted to wear and how she wanted to appear as a woman; that is what is so attractive about her. Although our styles are completely different – my techniques create structure and hers created looseness – we share a similar approach to fashion. We have no blueprint of what we intend to do. There is no grand seasonal plan. We create what we want to create. That is why I feel so very close to Chanel.

I remember perfectly my first experience of couture. During the '70s, there was a TV programme in France, every Wednesday, called *Aujourd'hui Madame*. And every season, during the haute couture shows, they would review the shows in Paris. It was very colourful that particular season, I seem to remember. It was most likely Paco Rabanne, Yves Saint Laurent and Pierre Cardin. You have to bear in mind that TV at the time, for a little kid like me, was like a window to the rest of the world, and the brightness of the colours and the girls and everything was something I couldn't completely comprehend. I remember thinking there must be some people who lived on the other side of my country who had an entirely different life to that of my parents. It was quite challenging in my mind. I was living in the Pyrenées. I was seven or eight. My father was a butcher. I was known as the son of the butcher. I guess I was supposed to also become a butcher.

If I say Coco Chanel is my most inspirational haute couturier from the past, then from the present it must be Karl Lagerfeld. I think when you work with the legacy of someone else it is so interesting to embrace it, whilst at the same time choosing to reject it, deform it or transform it. What Karl Lagerfeld is doing now for Chanel is referencing our time. He is taking the essence of Chanel, analysing the world as it is today, and creating designs that are relevant for our time.

If I had to choose one thing from history that I wish I had designed, it would be the corset. I wish I could have designed the very first one. Charles Worth was the first real couturier, and his house was behind the first corsetry. I would love to have designed it, to have understood it.

The technique that I find the most magical in the world of haute couture is the bias cut.

Roland Mouret
RM by the designer
Roland Mouret

"The bias cut turns the fabric to water. It allows the fabric to speak. You have to be humble when you work with the bias cut, because the fabric controls you and not the other way around"

Vionnet's work was so inspirational. What can I say? The bias cut turns the fabric to water. It allows the fabric to speak. You have to be humble when you work with the bias cut, because the fabric controls you and not the other way around.

My first experience of bias cutting was a nightmare, because everything I just said to you, I did the opposite. I thought that you could control it. I did not understand this concept of allowing the fabric to speak its own language. You have to accept its difference. You have to accept its touch. You have to acknowledge that you cannot predict the way the fabric is going to stretch between your fingers. You know, it's the same as skin – every skin is so different when you touch it – the same is true of fabric. The Vionnet dress that always sticks in my mind as the best example of bias cut is the four square handkerchief dress that she did in the '20s. The simplicity of it is so very challenging.

I have never experienced the couturiers' ateliers, and perhaps that's the beauty of my love for this job. I have no experience. I have never worked anywhere. I just went to the job by myself with my vision of changing things around me.

Fashion is still a young business. Couture is, what, 120 or 130 years old? And ready-to-wear is no more than 70 or 80 years old. You know, that's a short time – it's just the lifetime of a person. Every decade has become like a trend within itself. And the concept of luxury over the last 15 years has, in the end, become more of a lifestyle. This was most aptly expressed in the Valentino documentary *The Last Emperor*. When you examine the fashion world in the '70s and '80s in close detail, you realise that, back then, it was about selling clothes. Now it is about selling shares in your company. That's the way it works. The only similarity that remains is that you still need the same amount of love to make the company exist in the first place.

Couture is an amazing craft. There are amazing stories behind it. I don't agree with Christian Lacroix that "couture should be fun, foolish and almost unwearable". I think the world should be fun, foolish and almost unwearable. It would be a better place if it were. Couture does exist to make us dream. But unfortunately, you have to wake up every morning.

To be a true couturier today, you have to have been trained in the '20s – or at least taught by people who were trained in the '20s – in a way that is really no longer possible. The concept of couture is dying with the couturiers. The only way forward is for couture to go somewhere else.

These days, and actually since the beginning, the best fashion ideas come from a creative mind. There is no such thing as a fashion theme. Again, this is something that was dreamed up in

Left: This 1967 Paco Rabanne chain-mail dress combines Space-Age modernity with the look of medieval armour. Rabanne's use of unusual materials such as plastic, paper and aluminium would go on to inspire later avant-garde designers such as Helmut Lang. Rabanne also designed the wardrobe for Jane Fonda in 'Barbarella'

Below: A tweed coat and trousers designed by Pierre Cardin and modelled in Paris in July 1970

Opposite: Mouret's repertoire of signature figure-enhancing dresses has been augmented by cleverly constructed suits and coats in tweed and velvet for Autumn/ Winter 2010

the '70s to create big business. Designers do what they think women want to see in their wardrobes. Buyers and magazines make a theme of it, you know, to sell more. But that does not make it real. Chanel used her own body and sexuality to create clothes. The way she designed was the way she was dressing herself. She wanted to be loved. She designed clothes to be sexy. Her idea was that clothes were there to be taken off.

Apart from its inspirational value, couture in the 21st century is irrelevant. The beauty of couture was always in the service, and that's what we are missing. If you look at the work of Nicolas Ghesquière at Balenciaga, or Lee McQueen, they have been doing the quality of couture in their ready-to-wear for the past decade. Their showpieces are unique. True couture – where you go for five or six fittings to get the precise cut – the new clients don't want that. They don't get that. They want something now. They are living in the world of now. It's a more rapid world. The world of haute couture is in transformation. It will disappear, and then reinvent itself.

Biographical Notes

Roland Mouret was born in Lourdes, France in 1962. In 1979 he trained for three months at a fashion school in Paris, then worked as creative director for a Paris-based magazine while modelling for Jean Paul Gaultier. He later worked as a stylist for French *Elle* and *Glamour*. Mouret debuted his own collection at London Fashion Week in February 1998; he won British Designer of the Year at the 2002 *Elle* Style Awards, and was nominated for the same prize at the British Fashion Awards in 2004.

He is renowned for his deft ability to drape and for his form-flattering dresses, which embrace and enhance a woman's curves. For his Spring/Summer 2006 collection, Mouret created the iconic hourglass Galaxy dress. Its popularity among Mouret's A-list clientele turned him into a household name.

In 2006, Mouret parted company from his financial backers and formed the new brand, called RM by the designer Roland Mouret, with Simon Fuller's 19 Entertainment. He presented his first RM collection in Paris in July 2007.

Also in 2007, he created the Moon dress, which was another sellout success – this time made famous by Victoria Beckham. Mouret's dresses have also been worn by Sienna Miller, Keira Knightley, Scarlett Johansson and Rachel Weisz.

In 2010 he launched his debut menswear line, Mr by the designer Roland Mouret.

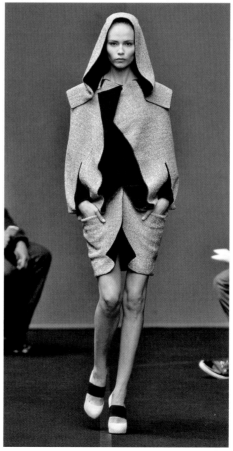

FASHION WAS NOT AN EASY FIT for me. I assume it was part of my imagination as a child. Like any little girl, I probably thought about fashion rather too much. My mother particularly favoured Jean Patou. I don't know why. That was my first experience of couture.

I grew up in the '60s, when society was becoming obsessed with consumerism. I suppose in reaction to that, I developed ideas about moral regeneration. I had dreams to stand up for equality and justice. I was a Communist but, at that point, being left-wing was fashionable, and I ended up being not so very different from thousands of other middle-class kids. A career in fashion was just about the least feminist path I could have taken – not at all useful, or so I thought at the time. Nevertheless, I liked it. But it took a lot of courage to get heavily involved in my family's business. Now I understand the fashion business. When people think about fashion, they only see the crazy side, the clichéd side – and actually all that is wrong. Fashion is an important part of a woman's life. It's all about personal aesthetics, and that is in no way stupid or superficial. What you wear is an expression of how you think. It should not be external, but a part of you. And I mean that for society as a whole. Both men and women want to embellish themselves, to express themselves creatively.

There is not one particular couturier that I liked from the last century. I have a very contemporary approach to design that I would say doesn't reflect the past at all. However, I have the greatest respect for all of the couturiers from history. They each loved fashion in different ways – each one loved different shapes, different colours.

The place of couture in society and the relationship between couturiers and their clientele was fascinating. But it's difficult for me to relate to them today. The time has changed. The places have changed. It's a different world. These days, you have not finished one collection before you start thinking about the next. Maybe it is all a little hysterical. It's a constant anxiety, which is probably a reflection of society's anxiety in general. But this big deal about newness in fashion – this frantic pursuit of originality – is very recent. It may be a good thing or a bad thing. I don't know.

I think those traditional crafts still have a real value, but that is not the sole aspect of design for me. Much more interesting is a mix of different things, such as the research into fabrics, prints, and new textile machines. When this kind of innovation is combined with craftsmanship, that's when I really love my job. We place an awful lot of importance on technology. If you visit our production facilities, you will see how much effort we make to discover the latest innovations

Miuccia Prada
Prada

in fabrics and accessories. The future is more interesting than the past. I can't say I have ever had much of a sense of history or heritage at all, even though it is considered a selling point, even by my own company. The difference is that we actually do have a history, but those companies that don't, they just make one up anyway. Those companies don't interest me at all.

These days, I find that the most important aspect of fashion design is not technique, but ideas. Ideas are magical. And it's the flow of ideas that goes into the process that makes a difference. I'm not sure everyone gets what we do. For the classicists, we are thought to be too fashionable, and for the fashionable, we are thought to be too classic. And either way we are considered neither luxurious nor bourgeois enough.

This economic crisis forces us all to work harder and more efficiently, but ultimately the mood now is for meaning. It is those designers who put thought into their designs who will succeed. Luxury on its own is not enough. I have always thought that luxury is more to do with intelligence than price. I also think that the word "luxury" itself has been overused and abused, and that the real trend today is the search for something that immediately relates to the customer – something that they can make sense of. It could be art or music or experiences.

I think that, in the context of fashion, couture is a kind of luxury, but it is more about exclusivity than anything else. In general, couture amounts to one dress being made for one person. This is just one of many forms of fashion today.

I do not do couture; just to do a few ultra-sophisticated pieces for couture connoisseurs would be, for me, completely boring. If all I did all day, every day was to create four fabulous dresses for four fashion snobs, I would change jobs.

Maybe at first I wanted to be taken seriously by the fashion crowd. And even today I still want to be understood by the sophisticated elite, but I want to be louder than that. I am interested in communicating with the world by selling to many, many people. Therefore, if you don't shout, then your message will not get through. I consider that to be a far greater challenge than creating couture. So I have to deal with utter sophistication – because of course I love it – and with being in contact with the entire world. This is the challenge I find endlessly interesting.

All the research, the special fabrics, the embroideries, the structured silhouettes – all these things that we do are the same as couture. I think it is wrong to define couture as the only place for intense beauty and creativity. I truly believe that the biggest challenge in fashion is to make things that are wearable. It's the first and foremost characteristic of clothes. Believe me, I love

"The most important aspect of fashion design is not technique, but ideas. Ideas are magical. And it's the flow of ideas that goes into the process that makes a difference"

eccentricity and excess. I like working against clichés and against the obvious. I tend to subvert the origins of ideas as well as all the rules, but not to the point that you feel uncomfortable in a situation. But that is just my personal opinion.

I tend to watch old movies at home. One of my favourites is Alain Resnais' *Last Year in Marienbad*. It is a French art-house film from the '60s. The costumes were designed by Coco Chanel; they are so beautiful. For me, the black gown is a true fashion reference; but I hate to be precise about such things. I am more interested in society today. I want to know what people are thinking and what is happening right now. Of course, when I see old films, I feel a certain nostalgia for the past, and I may try to capture a glance or an impression, but no more than that.

What I do when I design – or try to do – is to redefine beauty for today. There has to be intelligence in my work. I'm against the idea of design being useless. I hate the thought that we are striving to make things more and more beautiful without any prior thought. I always search for a reason for something. Beauty as mere beauty does not interest me at all. If there is no sense to beauty, who cares? The most important thing is quality – but when I say quality, I mean quality of thinking.

Biographical Notes

In 1913, Mario and Martino Prada opened a leather goods shop in Milan named Fratelli Prada. Mario's daughter Luisia became his successor and ran Prada for two decades before her daughter Miuccia took over in 1978.

Miuccia was an unexpected successor, with a PhD in political science and no formal design training. With Patrizio Bertelli, she brought a cool, minimalist creativity to Prada designs with the launch of her first black nylon backpacks and totes in 1979. A shoe line was released in 1984, and the classic Prada handbag appeared in 1985.

Prada's first ready-to-wear collection appeared in 1989. In 1992 Prada launched a younger and more affordable line named Miu Miu, after her childhood nickname. By the end of the decade, Prada's portfolio of luxury brands included Helmut Lang, Jil Sander and Fendi, but these were sold by 2006.

Prada was awarded the Council of Fashion Designers of America award in 1993 and 1995. She is renowned for subverting standard ideas of what is sexy, and her intelligent, critically acclaimed designs have won fans including Uma Thurman, Chloë Sevigny and Cameron Diaz.

*Right and below:
Delphine Seyrig and
Giorgio Albertazzi
(below with Seyrig)
starred in the 1960s
art house movie 'Last
Year in Marienbad'
(1961), with costumes
designed by Coco
Chanel. Seyrig
wore four distinct
little black dresses
by Chanel in the film*

*Opposite: Prada's
Autumn/Winter 2010
collection took its
inspiration from the
late '50s and early
'60s. Models with
beehives wore high
necklines and full
cashmere skirts that
fell to the knee, paired
with thick cable-knit
wool stockings
and pointed shoes
decorated with bows.
Nipped-in waists and
pointed bras made
the décolleté the focal
point of the hourglass
silhouettes*

The House of Balenciaga

The undisputed king of cutting, Cristóbal Balenciaga, spent his career refining and refining to the point that his designs looked deceptively simple. Nothing could be further from the truth. His rigorous construction and artful creativity have never been surpassed, and to this day he is held as the most innovative cutter of all time. Balenciaga's name is still connected to a number of fashion details, including raised front hemlines, dolman sleeves, large buttons and a collar that sits on a band and stands away from the throat. His most famous period, when it is widely believed that he was at his most creative, was during the '60s, when he developed a trapeze line wedding gown in gazar that sums up his legendary formal simplicity.

1895: Cristóbal Balenciaga is born in Getaria, a fishing village in the Basque region of Spain. His mother is a dressmaker, so he learns to make clothes at an early age.

1907: Balenciaga begins an apprenticeship with a tailor in San Sebastián and Madrid.

1918: He opens his first fashion house in San Sebastián, under the name House of Balenciaga; he quickly wins the patronage of the royal family and gains a reputation in Paris.

1931: The Spanish monarchy falls and Balenciaga is forced to find a new clientele. The name of the house is changed to Eisa, Balenciaga's mother's name.

1936: The Spanish Civil War forces the closure of Balenciaga's three Spanish outlets. Balenciaga tries to find work at Charles Worth and Maggie Rouff.

> "You are lucky. If you want to produce a masterpiece, you do it on your own. I need five hundred people to do it..."
> **Cristóbal Balenciaga to the surrealist painter Joan Miró**

1937: Balenciaga leaves Spain and, with the financial help of expat friends, sets up a new couture house in Paris on Avenue George V.

1938: Paris opens its arms to Balenciaga. His collection is a huge hit and, building on the success, Balenciaga creates the dresses worn by Hélène Perdrière in the film *Trois de Saint-Cyr*.

1939: The business expands to include an adjacent building and, at a presentation of his collection, the crowds fight to get in.

1940: The house reduces its workload as the war takes its toll on Paris.

1941: A collection of Spanish Renaissance-inspired dresses causes a sensation. The Spanish press reports that sales in the three Spain-based outlets are as high as ever.

1945: Balenciaga takes part in the Théâtre de la Mode with clothes modelled on dolls.

A collarless, polka-dotted smock top, 1951

Queen Fabiola's wedding gown, 1960

Double-breasted evening cape in white gazar, 1963

1946-1947: Embroidered boleros inspired by toreador jackets, and the Barrel collection are launched. As Dior debuts his New Look, American *Harper's Bazaar* editor Carmel Snow praises Balenciaga's seeming simplicity and rigorous construction.

1950: Balenciaga shows his first collarless pieces, including raincoats and blouses as well as balloon dresses.

1955: The first Balenciaga tunic debuts, in linen for summer, wool for winter and lace for cocktail wear. A year later, Balenciaga's signature capes and sack dresses first appear.

1958: Cristóbal Balenciaga is named Chevalier de la Légion d'honneur.

1959: Jackets become boxier and waistlines get higher.

1960: Balenciaga travels to Madrid to make Queen Fabiola of Belgium's bridal gown. This is the beginning of the period that most aficionados mark as Balenciaga's best, with austere designs that are at their most refined.

1962: Working with Mancini, the label launches its first range of boots.

1963: As the mood in fashion becomes more modern, Balenciaga creates a collection more suited to contemporary life, with tweed suits inspired by hunting costumes.

1967: Balenciaga creates the trapeze line wedding dress in white gazar with matching headdress. The press calls it "perfection".

1968: Balenciaga creates his last collection, which the press likens to a classic Rolls-Royce. He closes the House of Balenciaga and retires to Igueldo in Basque Spain. American socialite and Balenciaga devotee Countess Mona von Bismarck locks herself indoors for three days.

1972: Cristóbal Balenciaga dies, aged 77, and is buried in his native Basque country. The business passes to his nephews before being acquired and revived by the Groupe Jacques Bogart in 1986.

1992: Dutch designer Josephus Thimister replaces Michel Goma and begins re-establishing the brand.

1995: Nicolas Ghesquière joins the House of Balenciaga as a designer, becoming Creative Director for the label's ready-to-wear and accessories collections two years later. He revives the silhouettes pioneered by Balenciaga in the '50s and maintains a restrained palette for the house's signature style.

2001: Gucci Group acquires the House of Balenciaga.

2003: Kylie Minogue wears a Balenciaga minidress in the video for her No. 1 single *Slow*, as well as on tour.

2005: Ghesquière's Autumn/Winter collection impresses American *Vogue* editor Anna Wintour.

2006: The *New York Times* says of Ghesquière, "If he isn't the most important designer of his generation, it's hard to think who would be."

2008: Ghesquière's "liquid latex" look wows critics, and Balenciaga teams up with Coty to produce a new line of fragrances.

2010: Charlotte Gainsbourg, Ghesquière's friend and muse, becomes the face of the Balenciaga Paris fragrance. His Resort collection of 2011 is an homage to the airline uniforms that Balenciaga designed in the '60s. Ghesquière's colour palette is defined by something he calls "techno bohème" and includes iridescent shades and metallics.

"In a Balenciaga, you were the only woman in the room"
Diana Vreeland

Balenciaga by Henri Cartier-Bresson, 1968

Josephus Thimister's first collection, 1992

Nicolas Ghesquière, 2010

WHAT IS HAUTE COUTURE? I'm asking you. Because you know I haven't done haute couture since 2002. What I do is expensive ready-to-wear. Ready-to-wear is a very specific thing – they are clothes that you can buy in your size. Today you can count literally on one hand the true clients of couture. When I did my last couture collection for the house of Balmain, there were maybe 100 employees. At the time that Balmain was designing couture – back in 1946 – there were around 900.

Of course, I started my career in haute couture because I worked first for Balenciaga and then for Castillo at the house of Lanvin in Paris. We have to remember that haute couture was a craft that was made for the very few and the very privileged. That does not address the realities of couture for today. When I hear about designers saying things like "couture should be almost unwearable", then I know why they are out of business today. It's as simple as that.

When you create clothes, you have to think of the consumer. You have to know that ultimately there will be a victim who will fall madly in love with what you are doing; otherwise you shouldn't be doing it. Because it is only when a woman falls in love with something so much that she wants to wear it – it is at that point and that point only that it becomes fashion. What happens on the runway is not fashion – it is just spectacle. Fashion is once you say, "Gee, this will be great for me," and you decide to put it on because it will do something for you.

This is the most exciting time in history to be creating clothes, because never before have women been so in control of their own destinies. And obviously you have to address that woman. You have to understand her life and her lifestyle. If you don't, you are not a good designer.

Right now I am working on a show with the Spanish Institute in New York. It is a show of Balenciaga's work. There have been a lot of Balenciaga shows, and I have been talking to some of the people and some of the institutions that own some of Balenciaga's work. And when I phone these people, they always say, "Oh, I know where you can get the wedding dress he made for so and so. Or the evening gown that he made for someone else."

But that is not the kind of show I would like to make. Because I know what happens in an haute couture house, or at least what used to happen. A woman orders a dress. But her arms are maybe not so good, so she asks the saleslady helping her, "Well, instead of doing a short sleeve, can we do it down here? And I don't like this colour, so can you change it to another colour?"

So what happens is that the final dress is no longer the original concept of the designer; it is

Oscar de la Renta

"This is the most exciting time in history to be creating clothes, because never before have women been so in control of their own destinies"

the woman's concept. When I was first working at the house of Castillo at Lanvin, I was called to a fitting room where a lady was ordering some clothes. She wanted to make alterations to the original designs that Mr Castillo had drawn, and I had to sketch every single change that she was making to the dress.

She said, "I want the sleeve here, and I want the waist lower," and all this. And, eventually, after two hours, when I had sketched every single one of her changes – and it had begun to creep into my lunch hour – I said to the lady, "Well, if you don't like it this much, why don't you just go somewhere else?"

I was very young. The saleswoman went to talk to the head of the house to tell him how unbelievably rude I had been, and I was very firmly told, "The client is always right." That is a lesson that every couture designer needs to learn. What you should do is try to please the client without compromising yourself.

Unfortunately, couture has become a dying art. When I started, way back in the late '50s and early '60s, fashion houses that were doing ready-to-wear were going to Paris to get inspired by what the couture houses were doing, and then going back and translating that into ready-to-wear. Today there are an awful lot of extremely talented designers who understand that ready-to-wear will satisfy most consumers. You can make very exciting ready-to-wear clothes now at almost any price. This is what I do. It is expensive, but it is most certainly not haute couture – well at least not the haute couture that is in my mind.

Haute couture is a custom-made garment. It is specifically made for a client. There are perhaps two or three houses left in Paris, and I know most of the clients personally. Today the houses that make haute couture don't make couture to sell couture, they make it to sell other products. They do extravagant collections that no one wants to put on, and they sell perfume, cosmetics, and lots of other things – but they are not selling couture.

I don't know if this is true – and I hope it's not – but I heard a story about a designer who made an haute couture evening dress for a lady for €1m. And when this young lady was having her last fitting, she asked if the designer would come down and see her in the dress, and she was told that it wasn't included in the price. If that were me, and I was doing that for her, I would crawl to get to her. This is unbelievable.

Couture is a global business. It's a very competitive business. And today you are addressing a consumer who knows a great deal, and it is necessary to understand that consumer. A lot of the haute couture dresses that have been offered to me for this Balenciaga show are oversized – a lot of the ladies who wore couture back then were a size 16, and I don't want to have to pinch them in at the front and the back. Today, women who can afford couture tend to look after themselves, and keep themselves in shape.

Modern designers work in very different ways now. I still work in the way that I learned my craft. If I decide on a design, I give it to my people in the workroom, most of whom I have been working with for a very long time. If I gave my design to 10 different ladies and asked them to make up the dress, each of them would make a different dress. A sketch is just an idea, and it is only your dress when you start manipulating it yourself.

I remember being with my first wife who, at the time, was editor of French *Vogue*, and I went with her to have lunch with Mademoiselle Chanel, who looked at her suit, and it was a Chanel suit, and said, "Which one of my staff made this suit?" We quickly realised that Chanel was not happy with the standard of the suit, and my wife, who was always very impatient at standing for three hours at the fittings, didn't want to compromise the lady who had made the suit. Meanwhile, Mademoiselle Chanel started to pull at the sleeve and refit it herself. That is the way a proper couturier works.

Do I admire the current couturiers? Who are the current couturiers? I like what Lagerfeld does. When he started at Chanel, he was given something quite wonderful. Chanel was a great designer. She was a woman, and she designed for herself. She had a tremendous sense of style. She was one of the greatest designers of the 20th century, because she understood what the modern woman was about. She rid women of a lot of cumbersome things like corsets, and she was a rebel.

I think Cristóbal Balenciaga was a great designer because he was like an architect. He used to say, "You don't have to have a body; I will make one for you." But that is not the modern concept of clothes.

Fashion has evolved, and you should not look back; you should always look forward. The woman I was dressing when I first started working no longer exists today.

I have seen a lot of Balenciaga shows. He started his first fashion house in Spain, and the house went bankrupt. And he was never allowed, from then on, to use the name Balenciaga in Spain – that's how the bankruptcy laws work there. But even after going to Paris and becoming a huge success, I think that probably the best clothes he made were in the late '50s and '60s, just before the house closed. He remained very Spanish throughout, and the country's culture, art and folklore had a huge influence on his work.

One of the greatest Balenciaga customers

Left: Two tulle dresses
from Lanvin-Castillo,
photographed by
Henry Clarke for
French Vogue in April
1957. The black-and-
white dresses have a
strapless bodice with
a built-in corset
attached to a skirt
made of layers of stiff
tulle over a crepe
petticoat. De la Renta
worked at Lanvin-
Castillo at the
beginning of his
career. Antonio
Castillo was head
designer at the house
of Lanvin from 1950
to 1962, after being
hired by Jeanne
Lanvin's daughter

Opposite: A classic
Chanel suit in
oatmeal wool with
navy blue facings,
photographed in
Paris in 1959.
Chanel had only
returned to France –
and to haute couture –
in 1954, at the age
of 71, after a decade
of retirement and
self-imposed exile
in Switzerland.
Her collarless,
open box jackets,
piped in contrasting
colours, were hugely
successful in the '50s,
and would become
the "uniform" of chic
women worldwide

Left: A black-and-white strapless gown embroidered with net and crystals, by Balenciaga, ca 1951. Photographed by John Rawlings

Below: A pink silk full-skirted gown with a raised front hem, by Balenciaga, 1957. Illustration by Bernard Blossac

Bottom: A polka-dot black-and-white strapless gown with tiered skirt, by Balenciaga, 1946. Illustration by Pierre Mourgue

Opposite: Gowns from Oscar de la Renta's Autumn/Winter 2010 (bottom left) and Resort 2011 collections

was a lady called Mrs Gloria Guinness. She was Mexican and married to Loel Guinness, an Englishman. I remember hearing about Mrs Guinness when I was working for Castillo and through the years at Balenciaga. She used to buy a lot of clothes from Castillo. So one time, when I knew she was going to be having lunch with Castillo, I took my lunch hour a little bit earlier so that I could follow them. She was extraordinary. First of all very beautiful, but also very stylish. She had a beautiful suit with a pillbox hat and gloves up to here. But you know, people just don't dress that way anymore.

> "When a woman falls in love with something so much that she wants to wear it – it is at that point and that point only that it becomes fashion"

Biographical Notes

Oscar de la Renta was born in Santo Domingo in the Dominican Republic in 1932. At 18, he left for Spain, where he studied painting at the Academy of San Fernando in Madrid. He then began sketching for leading Spanish fashion houses, which led to an apprenticeship with Cristóbal Balenciaga.

He left Spain to work for Castillo at Lanvin, in Paris, and in 1963 he moved to New York, where he began designing clothing and accessories for some of the most prestigious fashion houses, including Elizabeth Arden. He launched his own label in 1965 and became well-known for sparking the gypsy and Russian trends of the '70s.

From 1973 to 1976 he was President of the Council of Fashion Designers of America (CFDA), and he created the CFDA Awards. In 1990, he was honoured with the organisation's Lifetime Achievement Award; he won two more CFDA awards, for Womenswear Designer of the Year, in 2000 and 2007.

From 1993 to 2002 de la Renta was also head couturier at Pierre Balmain; he was the first American to design for a French couture house.

Scarlett Johansson, Anne Hathaway, Hillary Clinton, Cameron Diaz and Eva Mendes are fans of de la Renta's dresses.

SO MANY DESIGNERS reference the work of Yves Saint Laurent. Whenever we talk about couturiers from the past, it is vital to put them into the context in which they worked. When Yves Saint Laurent was at Dior, working the crocodile leather jacket or playing with silhouette and volume, it was extremely groundbreaking. And when he put women in Le Smoking and elevated the safari jacket from a street piece into a luxurious couture garment, it had an incredible influence on fashion. He was also behind Rive Gauche and the prêt-à-porter side of things. For me, he epitomises what couture is all about.

If I had to single out one outfit that I wish I had designed, it would be the Bar suit by Christian Dior. I love the purity of it, how graphic it is – particularly the jacket. But it is also the total look. The silhouette of the skirt and the hat as well. Dior was a one-man fashion revolution.

I was pretty young when I first discovered couture – nine or 10. There were so many more shows then. Now, blink and you miss them. My grandmother used to pass on the fashion pages from *The Lady* magazine or *Country Life*. I remember seeing Karl Lagerfeld's designs for Chloé – not couture, I know, but I loved it, even though I wasn't sure how to pronounce Chloé.

I am incredibly lucky to have worked for Christian Lacroix. It was quite by chance. I had a Saturday job in The Conran Shop while studying at the Royal College of Art, and one weekend he came in with his wife. And I thought, oh my God, I can't let this go by. So when he left I ran after him and introduced myself, and said, "Can I come and do work experience with you?". And he said, "Well, send me a letter", which I did the following Monday. A month or two later I was called by the directrice of the haute couture salon, who asked if I was available to work in Paris on the couture collection. Did I expect to ever hear from him? No, absolutely not.

My job there was more as an observer. I had to draw every outfit in the collection to make a book for the couture clients. And sometimes, if a jacket had been designed to be worn with trousers, I was asked to create some skirts to show how it would look; or I would adapt an evening dress into a wedding dress. It was a fantastic job. I would sit in the studio while Mr Lesage came to show him the embroideries. It was an amazing education, a magical experience, and I guess it cemented the desire for me to stay and work in Paris.

Who would I like to have worked with? Cristóbal Balenciaga. He was a master of technique, volume and new fabrications. Even through the '60s, Balenciaga continued to be groundbreaking. His work was always to do with volume. His shapes and proportions were,

Peter Copping
Nina Ricci

"You can see the passion in couture pieces; you can sense the love that has constructed it. Couture is the polar opposite of an industrial process"

and still are, incredible. Schiaparelli, I love the whole fun aspect of it. The people that she collaborated with were fantastic, and there was always a modernism to what she designed. There was a small exhibition recently of her work that Azzedine put together. There were some really interesting pieces in it: simple black dresses with beautiful cuts and an interesting use of zips. She was one of the first designers to start using zips. Where would we be without zips?

With Dior, it's the whole fantasy thing. I'm always drawn back to the '50s, obviously, with Balenciaga as well. And with Courrèges, it's the purity that I really like, and his singular vision. I saw some Courrèges coats recently from the '60s, and they still look fabulous. I wonder if one gets drawn to the period in which one grows up. Because I was born in the '60s, I seem to always go back there for inspiration.

When you look at some of the amazing couture ball gowns, you see the construction that goes into them. I like the whole process of making up the toiles and building upon the ideas. The *petites mains* are passionate and meticulous, and I think you can see the passion in couture pieces; you can sense the love that constructed it. Couture is the polar opposite of an industrial process. The desire to have something that is not available en masse is what drives the new trend for luxury.

There are so few houses doing real couture at the moment. But then ready-to-wear is moving towards couture. At Nina Ricci, we have ready-to-wear dresses that retail at €15,000 that sell easily. Before, if people were spending that amount of money, they would expect to go to the house for five or six fittings; they would expect that level of service. Now, I'm not sure that women have the time. The process seems to be outdated.

Chanel has had the most lasting influence on fashion, for the modernity of her pieces. So many people have derived inspiration from the Chanel aesthetic. She had a real vision for clothes – a very challenging vision. Some of those suits are pared down to their simplest form. Jewellery and accessories get added, but some of her little tweed suits are just perfection in the way they were made. They have a real simplicity.

Couture is fashion in its purest and most exaggerated form – fashion that is pushed to the limit. But there are some fashion houses where the clothes are fantastic, but the context of the shows is too extreme. There are fashion houses that don't mind what gets produced so long as it's super-high-profile and it gets them publicity. Couture has become all about an extreme image, and part of the craftsmanship has got lost along the way.

I think we have Karl and Chanel to thank for

Right: Yves Saint Laurent's Porcelaine dress from his legendary Trapeze collection from Spring/Summer 1958

Below: Evening dresses by Christian Dior for a spring fashion show in Paris in February 1951

Opposite: The Autumn/Winter 2010 collection by Peter Copping was his official debut for Nina Ricci and saw a return to delicate femininity for the label. With an emphasis on sheer and satin fabrics as well as obviously hand-crafted details, the cool palette of silver, grey and black was lifted by hints of pretty pinks and appliquéd posies of roses. It's a resolute move away from Olivier Theyskens' vision for the brand, and one that seems to sit favourably with his new generation of fans

maintaining the artisanal houses like Lemarié and Massaro. All these amazing craftspeople who Karl encouraged Chanel to invest in are now part of Chanel. When you look at a Chanel show, it can be extreme, but there is always a reality. However over-the-top, Karl's designs are always desirable. Chanel is the only house that is really doing couture.

I was really inspired by Karl when I started out. I can remember seeing his early work. I loved his personality. The first collections he did for Chanel in the mid-1980s were amazing. He has a respect for the artisans. He knows what to do with the things they create.

There is a real need for things to feel special in fashion right now. There's a real place for couture. I wouldn't like to see it being overtaken by big companies to be used for communication. We need to encourage new people to get involved with it. The Chambre Syndicale is very rigorous; there are so many constraints. You have to employ a certain number of people. So you have all the expense of that on top of the expense of putting on a show and creating a collection. They may have to rethink things a bit.

> ## "There is a real need for things to feel special in fashion right now. There's a real place for couture"

Biographical Notes

Maria "Nina" Ricci was born in Italy but moved to France, where she worked as a dressmaker in Paris; she founded the Nina Ricci fashion house in 1932 at the age of 50. Ricci's perfume L'Air du Temps was launched in 1948 and continues to be a top seller.

Peter Copping was born in Oxford and graduated from both Central Saint Martins and the Royal College of Art. He is inspired by French design and has lived in Paris for 19 years.

After designing for Christian Lacroix, Sonia Rykiel and Marc Jacobs at Louis Vuitton – where he spent 12 years – Copping took over as Artistic Director of Nina Ricci in April 2009, replacing Olivier Theyskens.

Copping's 2009 unofficial debut established an aesthetic entirely at odds with Theyskens', and more in keeping with the original Nina Ricci signature. Ruffles, lace, embroidery and appliqué echoed the sophisticated styles from the '30s and '40s. Copping also designs accessories, leather goods and shoes. He launched his lace-covered black leather Ombre handbag for Nina Ricci in a limited edition of 10.

Elie Saab

IN THE '70s, LEBANON was a very fashionable place to be. There were stylish women out on every street, and I was like the fashion police – I was interested in fashion from a very early age. It felt as though I was born with it already inside me. Every time I saw anything connected with fashion and beautiful women, I was fascinated. I always had an opinion about the beauty of a woman. I would say, "she looks good" or "she isn't looking so good". Even as a seven-year-old, I was in the service of women.

I made my first dress for my sister when I was maybe 10 years old. It was a blue and white striped dress and I made it all by hand. I didn't have a sewing machine. And even if I'd had one, I wouldn't have known how to use it. But I was an early starter – I got my first sewing machine when I was about 12 years old.

I can't name one designer in particular who I think has had the most influence on fashion, because I believe that everyone in the pantheon of haute couture has contributed in some particular way. And I'd also have to say that there is not one single couture designer that has inspired me more than any other. Each one has their own identity, their own signature. Having said that, I have a huge amount of respect for Christian Dior – his vision, his development – and for Cristóbal Balenciaga, too. Coco Chanel had tailoring as her motif. Madame Grès was doing all the draping on the mannequin. And Givenchy brought all the glamour from the '50s. Each and every one has their place.

Glamour is very important to me, and I have the greatest admiration for fashion designers who have the most respect for the beauty of women. Karl Lagerfeld always respects women. Chanel is a house that I hold up as an ideal. It's a fantastic example of a fashion success story. The image of the House of Chanel has been very well maintained by Karl. And Valentino has always had a very good sense of the femininity of women. He was the most amazing couturier.

The one dress that I wish I had designed was the wedding dress for Grace Kelly that Helen Rose, the wardrobe designer at MGM, made for her as a wedding gift from the studio. It is just so simple, so beautiful.

The silhouette that can be created by traditional couture skills is the most interesting thing about couture for me. Of course I love all the details, like embroidery, and the work of the beading house of Lesage is very impressive. The story behind it is incredible, too. Under Albert Michonet, who sold it to Albert Lesage in 1924, it was once the embroiderer for Charles Worth, the founding father of haute couture. But femininity is my speciality, and construction is the key to that. Not too many designers have mastered the art of

construction. Christian Dior spent a lot of time on it, and Madame Vionnet mastered the bias cut. In my fashion house, I have some very good examples of the bias cut by Madeleine Vionnet.

One thing that has changed since her time is the fabrics; they are made differently today, with the help of technology. Nowadays, there are many types of silk that have been combined with other fibres and acetates. As a result of these developments, the fabric industry has altered the way that fashion works. We live life more easily than we did before. But as much as technology has brought about change, women's bodies haven't really changed. Admittedly, their shape has altered – if you look at the women of the last century, they were much softer. They had breasts! The female silhouette is now leaner and harder. But the art of creating clothes to fit the body hasn't changed. The art of creating a dress to perfectly follow the contours of the body, down to the very last millimetre, relies on skills that technology can't influence. Even the smallest detail counts. To make a minuscule alteration in one place can massively affect the overall look. Couture is architecture for the body.

I'm a self-taught designer – totally. From the very beginning, I worked to have my own style, to create my own way. I needed to discover everything with my own eyes. I was like a blank page. I had no preconceptions.

As a consequence, I've never worked with any other designer, so I don't really know how they work. The way I design relies on touch. First of all, I get a feel for the fabric; I weigh it up in my hands and feel the movement. I don't believe in sketching or designing. I work three-dimensionally from the start. I mould the fabric to the mannequin. My prototype dress is always made in the same fabric as the end result to get the best from the material. I make modifications on the body, but the creative process begins with me only.

Couture allows you to go far with your ideas. There is no limit, no ceiling to the budget. You can use embroidery and beading and too much fabric. You can dream. When we do prêt-à-porter we have to be careful, we have to be commercial. But I don't believe couture should be unreachable. Originally, my fashion house relied on haute couture so now, in my mind, if I design a dress, and it doesn't get ordered many times, then I'm very sad. Success, for me, is seeing my dresses being worn by many women. Then I am very happy. I don't believe that my creations should be destined for a glass cabinet or an archive. My job is to make women happy. More than financial gain, my impetus is to create beauty.

Couture and prêt-à-porter are two very different things. Couture is more artistic; there is more

"Even the smallest detail counts. To make a minuscule alteration in one place can massively affect the overall look. Couture is architecture for the body"

handwork, and it's about the details. It takes more than an ability to draw to make couture. You need such great vision. It is a different job. You also have to understand who the dresses are for. To build a collection, I need to have many muses in my head, as each collection must appeal to many types of women. I don't have one type in my mind. It's part of my culture to want to appeal to women all around the world.

The concept of couture has changed so much since Dior's day. It was during the '80s that the couture houses stopped thinking about the client. Couture became all about image. It stopped being about selling the clothes and started to become about selling accessories or perfume.

My house works more like how the old style of couture worked. I do couture for normal women with normal prices. It's less about spectacle and more about what a woman wants to wear. If a woman knows about couture – if she has an appreciation for couture – then she won't want to buy from a boutique. You feel different when you wear couture.

> ## "My job is to make women happy. More than financial gain, my impetus is to create beauty"

Biographical Notes

Elie Saab was born in July 1964 in Beirut, Lebanon. In 1981, he moved to Paris to study fashion but ended up returning to Beirut and opening up a workshop in 1982, when he was just 18 years old.

Saab was the first non-Italian to become a member of the Italian Camera Nazionale della Moda in 1997. He showcased his first collection in the same year in Rome and began a ready-to-wear collection in 1998. His first fashion show in Monaco was attended by Princess Stephanie.

Saab dressed Queen Rania of Jordan for her coronation in 2002, and Halle Berry wore one of his dresses when she picked up her 2002 Oscar for Best Actress.

Saab's style is for feminine couture dresses with brightly coloured silks, chiffons, pearl beading and embroidered lace. His range has also extended to bridalwear; for a Middle Eastern bride he designed a $2m classically styled dress with 2,000 carats of emeralds and 300 carats of diamonds.

Below: A gown from Valentino's Autumn/Winter 2007 collection – his last before his retirement in February 2008. The empire-line silk crepe gown has a ruched décolleté and a fishtail skirt, and is worn with a cape made of organdie petals

Top right: Grace Kelly in her fairy-tale wedding dress, which was made for her by MGM's costume designer, Helen Rose, when Kelly married Prince Rainier III of Monaco in 1956. Rose used antique lace, 25 yards of silk taffeta and 98 yards of tulle.

Bottom right: A strapless dress by Givenchy from 1955 with an inset boned bodice and a festoon tulle trim on the skirt

Opposite: Looks from Elie Saab's Autumn/ Winter 2010 haute couture collection: (clockwise from top

left) an asymmetric nude chiffon gown; the wedding gown, with lace guipure detailing, an eight-foot train and an embroidered tulle veil; a pleated scarlet georgette gown with draped folds; and a taupe tulle gown with embroidered ruffles

The House of Yves Saint Laurent

The image that Yves Saint Laurent's name conjures up is an elegant confection of feathers and chiffon. Yet his early collections for Christian Dior were often repudiated by the press and a somewhat conservative '50s clientele. The Beat Look of 1960 was about as far from traditional couture as you could get, and caused an outright scandal. Just a few years later, Saint Laurent returned to glamour and became a stalwart of the couture world until he retired in 2002. The ready-to-wear line came under the eye of Tom Ford in 2000 and, in 2004, Stefano Pilati, who has defined an original signature look.

1936: Yves Henri Donat Mathieu-Saint-Laurent is born in Oran, Algeria.

1948: Saint Laurent attends the Lycée d'Oran.

1953: He wins third prize in the International Wool Secretariat competition in Paris.

1954: He starts a design course at the École de la Chambre Syndicale de la Couture Parisienne and wins three out of four first prizes for the International Wool Secretariat competition. Karl Lagerfeld wins the fourth prize.

1955: Saint Laurent is hired as a design assistant to Christian Dior. One of his first designs, a white gown, is photographed by Richard Avedon for *Harper's Bazaar*. He works alongside Pierre Cardin.

> "I prepared that collection in a complete state of elation. I knew I was going to be famous"
>
> **Yves Saint Laurent, on his first collection for Dior**

1957: Dior dies suddenly of a heart attack and, after some deliberation, Saint Laurent is hired as his successor.

1958: Saint Laurent's triumphant Trapeze collection hits the right note, adhering to the Dior signature while moving the house in a more modern direction. Saint Laurent is introduced to Pierre Bergé, who will later become his life partner as well as his business partner. The second collection that year is less well received.

1959: The spring Long line meets with the approval of the house and the press, but the autumn collection's narrow skirts are unacceptable to the more conservative clients.

1960: In tune with the mood of the new decade, the Beat Look is a sophisticated take on the street styles of Parisian art students. Despite such ultra-luxurious fabrics as fur-trimmed leather and cashmere, the separates fail to seduce the house or its clients. Later in the year, Saint Laurent is conscripted into the army and, after falling ill, is despatched to a hospital to recuperate. Once he returns to Paris, he discovers that Marc Bohan has been brought back from Dior's London operation and made head of the house. Distraught, Saint Laurent decides to set up his own couture house.

Yves Saint Laurent in his Paris studio, 1963

The Mondrian dress from 1965

Saint Laurent dresses Catherine Deneuve, 1966

1961: Bergé finds a millionaire American backer and rents a property in the 16th arrondissement in which to set up the new house.

1962: On 29th January, Saint Laurent launches his couture house with a much-lauded collection that wins back many of his fans. For the next few years, he cements a signature style that translates everyday garments into super-luxe fabrics.

1965: The Mondrian dresses restore his popularity with the press and elegantly fuse art with fashion, which satisfies Saint Laurent's intellectual aspirations. He also designs the costumes for Catherine Deneuve's role in *Belle de Jour*.

1966: Le Smoking takes off and is reprised many times in Saint Laurent's lifetime. The autumn collection is inspired by Saint Laurent's new friend, Andy Warhol. A prêt-à-porter boutique opens called Rive Gauche.

1968: A see-through chiffon dress trimmed with ostrich feathers causes a sensation, as does the Safari look, captured by Franco Rubartelli on Veruschka in August 1968.

Saint Laurent outside his London store, 1969

1969: The Rive Gauche men's range is launched. Although at first Saint Laurent is behind the modernity of ready-to-wear, he reveals to friends that he is considering giving up fashion design.

1970: Throughout the late '60s and early '70s, Saint Laurent is seen as part of the international jet set, attending parties at Studio 54 in New York and Regine's in Paris.

1971: Saint Laurent gives up designing couture to concentrate on the ready-to-wear collections.

1972: Loulou de la Falaise joins the house as Saint Laurent's muse. She has a good eye, and helps to select the ready-to-wear looks.

1973: He relaunches his couture collection, allowing him creative freedom once more. He returns to the cycle of four collections per year. He also increases his theatrical work, designing costumes for Jean-Louis Barrault's stage version of *Harold and Maude*.

1974: Saint Laurent revisits the classic aesthetic that he favoured early on in his career and establishes an elegant, sophisticated signature that lasts for his lifetime.

1976: Léon Bakst's elaborate costume designs for the Ballets Russes inspire the Autumn/Winter couture collection, which receives rave reviews. Saint Laurent's health is suffering due to exhaustion.

From YSL's haute couture collection, 2000

1977: YSL's new fragrance, Opium, causes a sensation, with its provocative ad campaign making headlines.

1983: Saint Laurent is honoured by Diana Vreeland after she curates a retrospective of his career at the Metropolitan Museum of Art in New York. He is the first living artist or designer to have a solo show there.

1999: Gucci buys a controlling stake in Yves Saint Laurent and later installs Tom Ford as Creative Director of ready-to-wear.

2002: Saint Laurent retires, taking the couture line with him.

2004: Stefano Pilati takes over the design of the label's ready-to-wear.

2008: Saint Laurent dies in Paris.

> "Why Yves Saint Laurent? Because he is a genius, because he knows everything about women"
> **Diana Vreeland**

Stefano Pilati on the runway in 2010

Marios Schwab

I WAS VERY ARTISTIC when I was young, and I drove my parents crazy. I drew pictures all over my schoolbooks, in the margins. And the school was always complaining. I was the kind of child that just draws the whole time; I drew bodies and people, mainly – the people who were around me at the time.

When I said to my parents, "I just want to get out of here. I want to do what I'm passionate about," they agreed. They did their research and found a school in Austria which was like a finishing school. In fact, it was a very traditional girls' school where you learn these sewing techniques and things – either as life skills, to turn you into the perfect wife, or for a profession. The traditional skills they taught were surprisingly technical. We learned the trade, from basics to pretty hard-core. We went into all the detail of French tailoring, English tailoring and Italian manufacturing.

It was strangely intense, and the first month it was awful. I was the only boy in the class – well, the only boy in the school. I was really homesick, and I kept crying because there was one teacher who constantly made us re-stitch our seams if they weren't absolutely perfect. If she looked at the back of the garment, and it wasn't just as beautiful as the front, she'd make you open up the seams and redo the whole thing.

The way we were taught pattern cutting was the proper couture way – draping on the dummy. It was terribly complicated, but it's the right way. Can you imagine all these 60-year-old ladies teaching all these 15-year-olds, and being so very specific? I can remember thinking, I don't really need to know this. When am I ever going to need that? Because it was all these old-fashioned hand techniques.

But you know, actually, that training has had a huge impact on me. Now, so many years later, I always go back to that way of working. I may have modernised the details, but that ethic of working provides a kind of base to everything I do. I always start by draping on the mannequin. I show it to the pattern cutters and they take it away and make it functional – it becomes a flat pattern. Actually, what I learned at school were all the traditional techniques that are associated with couture. We had to learn Austrian cording techniques and how to achieve raised patterns on the surface of the fabric. We had this amazing technique using two layers of fabric – duchesse satin and chiffon on the back. We would stitch tiny motifs with a special machine, then cut through the chiffon at the back and feed wadding into the space. So on the surface you would make an anaglyph.

There is a subtle modernity to all Cristóbal Balenciaga's pieces. Whenever I visit Paris, I go to the vintage stores to search out his work. The shape, the sculptural element, is always contemporary and enduring. He is a minimalist, in a way, while he is doing the ultimate in luxury – I find that very inspiring. The sculptural element together with the surprise details – when you turn around the garment you always see something very attractive, some hidden detail to discover.

My favourite Balenciaga dress had a squared shape – a high neck and no sleeves. It is very sculptural. Most of the dresses that he designs are ultra-elegant. Even when he designs in pastel colours, the sculptural silhouette takes it away from being sweet and it becomes terribly sophisticated. Vintage couture Balenciaga seems to adapt itself to whoever is wearing it. Sophisticated sculpture is signature Balenciaga. I love Balenciaga now, too. Nicolas Ghesquière is such a visionary. He's incredible.

Schiaparelli, together with Dalí, took surrealism to another level – to a fashion level. What I love to think about when I create something is to always incorporate the body in what I am covering it with. There needs to be correspondence between the body and the clothing. Since I first saw the skeleton dress by Schiaparelli, I have always come back to it. I show it to pattern cutters to explain to them how to exaggerate something whilst still being minimal. Both the back and the front of the dress have the skeleton motif.

I believe in collecting things. If you love it, you should collect it. I don't like the thought that you buy something one season and then you give it away then next – or throw it away. I like to imagine that you buy something and put it away in your wardrobe and some time later you rediscover it like a lost treasure. This is a major inspiration in my work. I always return to the past – to nostalgia. You will always see in my work the same elements that were apparent throughout my childhood, and the evolution through my youth.

The women in my life have had a huge influence over what I now do. When I think back to my education, I have mixed emotions. It was a very difficult thing for a 15-year-old. But I was incredibly fortunate. My family recognised my passion.

I was a hyperactive child. I was also quite obsessive about things like my mum's tin boxes full of buttons, or threads or antique tape measures. I was lucky that my mum and my auntie were into fashion. They used to travel a lot to Italy to get fabrics. Both of them made many of their own clothes – particularly my aunt, who even made tailored pieces. She was quite voluminous, but in a sexy way – like Gina Lollobrigida. She loved devoré fabrics. When

"It is mind-blowing that the couture ateliers are still there – that there are still people who are skilled enough to create these extraordinary gowns"

I look now at the fabrics they bought, and compare them to what is available on the market today, I wonder what changed. Where did all those incredible silks go? They had things like a silk that was devoré on one side and a completely different pattern on the underside. It was a highly refined fabrication.

These days, my mum and auntie have really slowed down. They don't make their clothes anymore. Somehow fashion seemed more exciting back then.

I admire Vionnet so much, because the cut is immaculate. Whenever I think of an ultra-luxurious garment, Vionnet springs to mind. I love minimal garments with some special detail that makes them very desirable. The way of cutting that Vionnet invented was minimal but the seaming details, the layering, was all logical – and inspirational.

I find it fascinating to look at designers from the past who cut in a logical way – when you just think of fabric as one piece, like the petal of a flower wrapping around a body. That is very similar to the way that Cristóbal Balenciaga worked. Layering was the way that he achieved such incredible shapes.

Both Galliano and Karl Lagerfeld are such dreamers. Neither has retained the signature look of the house as it stood. But they have made it equally special. I remember one show from Galliano that really struck me at the time. It was inspired by Geisha. The fabrics were just incredible. It was perfect. The cut of the clothes was quite simple, but the fabrics were incredible and the colours all worked together to create an amazing effect. It was breathtaking.

On the other hand, Karl Lagerfeld creates a kind of perfect refinement. Whenever I see his couture clothes, I'm struck by how the garments move. It is this detail that I find most fascinating. He has obviously thought about that. It is very special; it takes real artistry to create that.

Couture is not just about pattern cutting, it's also about understanding the material – and how you position it and construct with it. It is mind-blowing that the couture ateliers are still there – that there are still people who are skilled enough to create these extraordinary gowns. This is what couture is: pieces of art. With any collection from Karl, there's always something that is totally beautiful.

I don't look at vintage pieces for creative inspiration. But I do love to look at the technical side. I love to have a real garment in my hands so that I can dissect its construction – I can turn it inside out and see how it has been made.

But when it comes to design, I think it is crucially important to reflect the times in which we are living. References are great – they give

*Opposite, top:
A bias-cut silk jersey
Madeleine Vionnet
dress photographed
for the cover of the
September 1934 issue
of Votre Beauté, at
a time when her
influence, popularity
and creativity were
at their peak*

*Opposite, bottom:
Fashion illustrator
Jean Pages' artwork
from 1932, depicting
a range of models
wearing the latest
designs by (from left)
Marcel Goupy, Elsa
Schiaparelli, Rose
Descat, E'Ahetz,
Lyolene, Vera Borea,
Schiaparelli again,
and Coco Chanel*

*Right: Photographed
by Hiro, the Harper's
Bazaar staff
photographer from
1956 to 1975,
Balenciaga's
four-sided cocktail
dress was fashioned
from black gazar –
a stiffer form of silk
developed on request
by Balenciaga because
of the way it held its
shape. It was made
for his 1967 collection,
the year before "the
Garbo of fashion"
closed the doors on his
fashion house forever*

Above left, centre and right: Marios Schwab's own-label collection for Autumn/ Winter 2010, inspired by his nostalgia for the Annahof Schule in Salzburg, the traditional girls' finishing school where he was a pupil

Left and right: Marios Schwab's debut Autumn/Winter 2010 collection for Halston included shades of putty, grey and rose juxtaposed with jewel tones.

His inspiration was the 1978 film, 'The Eyes of Laura Mars' with Faye Dunaway

Opposite: Elsa Schiaparelli's skeleton dress from 1938. Created in black silk crepe with plastic zips, and with the "bones" stuffed with cotton wadding, at the time it was considered an affront to good taste. Schiaparelli and Dalí also made the famous lobster dress, worn by the Duchess of Windsor

the mood or they give you the style – but when it comes to developing a garment, I love to sit down with the pattern cutters and take the fabric in my hands and translate it into something for a different world.

I believe that leaving a trace of yourself is the purpose of life. By involving myself in the craft of fashion, I believe I am leaving something of myself behind.

"When it comes to developing a garment, I love to sit with the pattern cutters and take the fabric in my hands and translate it into something for a different world"

Biographical Notes

Marios Schwab was born in Athens in 1978 to a Greek mother and an Austrian father. After studying fashion at ESMOD in Berlin, he moved to London and took a job in the studio of fashion label Clements Ribeiro.

Schwab completed an MA in Womenswear Fashion at Central Saint Martins, studying under the guidance of Louise Wilson.

He worked for designer Kim Jones before starting his own business. In 2005, he launched his own label and made his debut at London Fashion Week for Spring/Summer 2007.

Schwab won the prize for Best New Designer at the British Fashion Awards in 2006; he also won the Swiss Textiles Award in 2007.

His Spring/Summer 2008 show was chosen as one of the top 10 collections by Style.com.

In 2010, Schwab showed his first collection for the American brand Halston at New York Fashion Week.

Schwab is renowned for his esoteric and intellectual inspirations – Pythagoras and geology have provided the starting points for previous collections – from which he creates sculpted and figure-accentuating dresses, with unusual silhouettes.

Schwab's designs have been worn by Kylie Minogue, Chloë Sevigny, Kate Moss, Clémence Poésy and Thandie Newton.

Paul Smith

I CAN'T DO A FAVOURITE, SORRY. I always have a problem with the word "favourite". Like what is your favourite music? Or what is your favourite city? It's subjective. Paris is romantic. New York and Tokyo are full of energy. My favourite music right now might be opera, but if I wanted to be more relaxed, maybe I would choose something else. A favourite is a tough call.

But if I were being more specific than favourite – if I were saying which designer could have really taught me something, for example – then that would be Balenciaga. He was a genius at draping on the stand – just pinning it on the stand. And I would say Yves Saint Laurent for his skill at taking couture into the modern age. And I would say Christian Dior for his dogged work throughout the war years, and then for coming up with something as radical as the New Look. Those skirts are so very right for now, don't you think? I love the work of Givenchy for Audrey Hepburn – those little, simple dresses that Hubert de Givenchy designed for her were lovely. Obviously she had the right figure; she was petite. She had very good posture, so they worked really well for her. But Balenciaga was the master of drape.

My wife and I were fortunate enough to go to many of the couture shows when they were still held in the small houses of the designers, with about 30 people in the audience. We did that for quite a lot of years.

Our era, I suppose, was all about Yves Saint Laurent, because back then he was still a young couturier. This was during the '80s and early '90s, when he was still designing couture, but it felt very modern. When he announced the closing of his couture house, I thought it would be lovely for my wife to have one of the couture Le Smoking suits made, because she had worn a ready-to-wear Le Smoking suit and always looked stunning in it. And she'd had the red fox coat and quite a few items from the ready-to-wear, but she had never had couture. So we did it.

There were three fittings, I think – it was kind of up to you and them. Le Smoking has quite a simple line, so maybe she just had two fittings and then the final pick-up. We worked with the head cutter there, who makes sure that she has all your measurements correct. It was a lovely experience. We have bespoke at my company, and I have a strong knowledge of tailoring already, so I guess it was more familiar territory for me and Pauline because we understand how things are constructed. But it was still terrific. And, of course, the quality of the fabric that they use, and the precise way they work, is a really lovely experience.

When my wife was a student at the Royal College of Art, they still taught couture skills. These days, students learn more about ready-to-wear. It's much more about image or marketing or networking. Back in our day, it was about how things are made, what's inside a garment, how you put a sleeve in, the pitch of the sleeve, the balance of the whole garment, how it sat on the body, how to pad-stitch a lapel to gradually round it by pulling the thread tighter each time, the difference between this type of interlining and that type of interlining. Because you can have a fine gauze interlining or you can have a horsehair one, which will give you either a very fluid construction or a stiffer one. And you can either ease a sleeve in gently with little puckers at the top, or you can put it in very cleanly.

That kind of skill they don't really concentrate on like they used to, because it's probably seen as quite old-fashioned. In my opinion, that's a bit like being an architect without having the formal understanding of structure and balance, or knowing whether or not something is going to stand up. If you have a proper understanding of tailoring, if you know about the foundations of fashion design, you can then do things that are a lot more modern and different. I was really fortunate that my wife passed on all that knowledge to me. She is the secret to my success. Absolutely. Without question.

Is it a shame that the old ways have changed? It's progress, isn't it? Modernity. I mean, here we are on this photo shoot today. It's all totally digital. You see the images on three screens immediately. It's amazing. But you could say it's a shame that you don't spend hours in the darkroom developing and printing the film. It's just the way things have moved forward. Yes, it's a shame. No, it's not a shame.

Fifty or 60 years ago, if you went across France and Italy and probably Britain, too, there would have been many shops selling fabric, because dressmaking – either making clothes yourself or getting a dressmaker in the local town to make something – was commonplace. Of course, as we've "progressed", with ready-to-wear, the whole thing has changed.

When I used to go to the shows, the interesting thing about couture was the fact that, in the audience, there would be a few debutantes, maybe a rock star – or pop star as they were called in those days – but in total only around 20 or 30 people. It was also commonplace to see in the audience a couple of nuns from a convent somewhere in France, with a tribe of young girls. Because, back then, couture was considered a very important career. And they were all there to observe something called "couture" with a view to becoming an embroiderer, a lacemaker or a seamstress. Couture was an industry, and a very serious one.

But as ready-to-wear has come along, a lot of the couture houses have stopped. And because we

"For the process of couture – which is amazing, gorgeous and fantastic – you have to be patient, because it's craftsmanship, and it takes longer"

113

Left: Yves Saint Laurent's 1966 Le Smoking tuxedo for women morphed into a three-piece suit the following year, when this photo was taken. Le Smoking anticipated the power suit, the pant suit and other androgynous styles for women, and YSL's empowerment through tailoring had a profound effect on fashion and culture

Below: Audrey Hepburn wearing a Givenchy creation in the 1957 film 'Funny Face'. Hepburn and Givenchy's friendship began in 1953, when they worked together on 'Sabrina', and Givenchy's designs transformed the little gamine into a style icon. Although now regarded as a classicist, when he first arrived on the fashion scene in 1952, he was considered something of a trailblazer

Opposite: Paul Smith's Autumn/Winter 2010 collection was a playful take on English country house dressing and equestrian attire. It included organza dresses with rose prints, fine mohair knits and tweed suiting, paired with ripped fishnet stockings

want things instantly, like *now* – like my images on that screen *right now!* – we have all become so impatient. You sit in front of your computer on the Internet and you get angry because you can't find out how many types of tree there are in the world within 30 seconds. It's completely absurd. But that's the world we now live in.

So if you're going out for a dinner, and you need a dress, you go and you buy a dress. But for the process of couture – which is amazing and gorgeous and fantastic – you have to be patient, because it's craftsmanship, and it takes longer.

Unfortunately, couture just doesn't fit into today's world. It has become a very different type of industry now. It's much more about prestige, and probably quite a bit snob-related as well. The love of a particular designer and wanting to get closer to that designer because you might have the chance of meeting them – which is actually probably not going to happen, but at the very least you would experience visiting the house and having a garment that would fit your body – that's modern couture. If you have a complicated shape, then couture could be totally wonderful for you. But if you have a pretty simple body, with bumps in all the right places, then you can probably very easily get away with ready-to-wear. That's it.

"Unfortunately, couture just doesn't fit into today's world. It's much more about prestige, and probably quite a bit snob-related as well"

Biographical Notes

Sir Paul Smith was born in Nottinghamshire in 1946. He left school at 15 with the ambition to become a racing cyclist until his father made him get a job at a clothing warehouse.

After a cycling accident, Smith spent six months in hospital, and while recuperating, he began to make new, artistic friends. He took tailoring classes in the evenings and was hired by Savile Row's Lincroft Kilgour. His designs were worn by many celebrities, including George Best.

His girlfriend (now wife), Pauline Denyer, who is an RCA fashion graduate, helped him open his own shop in Nottingham in 1970. In 1976, he showcased his new Paul Smith menswear collection in Paris. In 1998, he showed his first women's collection at London Fashion Week.

Today there are 12 Paul Smith collections, including accessories, childrenswear, fragrance and furniture. Smith describes his style as "classic with a twist", English tailoring infused with a sense of wit and playfulness.

IF I COULD HAVE DESIGNED any one garment, it would be the Chanel suit. Not a bad little earner, eh? The great thing about that suit is that it allows the house to anchor itself. In fact, that suit is the ultimate anchor. So if you look at what Lagerfeld does with the couture shows, using that suit as a starting point, it always looks like Chanel. Even though he plays with the proportion a little bit – the skirt might be a little bit longer or shorter, the jacket could be more or less embellished – it still looks like Chanel. When you see the garments he creates and the beautiful way that he uses couture techniques, you can certainly feel Coco Chanel's overarching influence dragging him back to a point that is firmly rooted in her signature style. And the suit seems to have infinite scope for variation. God knows they must have made some money from that suit. The couture version is 10 times the cost of my ready-to-wear – and it's still just a suit.

Yves Saint Laurent's Trapeze collection is the most inspirational collection by any designer, making him, in my opinion, the most influential couturier in history. After arriving at Dior in 1957, within a very short time he was made head designer. It was an unusually confident move for a man in his twenties to produce something that was so simple and chic, and so very perfectly proportioned. It demonstrated that, even at that age, he had a fantastic handle on what made women look beautiful. When you study his later work and understand his real natural inclination towards theatrical clothes, I think it's incredible the way he managed to rein himself in at Dior, take his lead from the house, and produce a collection that was so very grown up. It showed an enormous amount of talent. He was genuinely precocious. You see so many young designers overcomplicating their work. It takes real confidence to do something so simple, and to execute it beautifully. That's what inspires me most. Later in his career, he expressed his talent in much more intricate, much more worked, much more colourful – much messier, even – pieces. But that early cut of those clothes inspires me to keep it simple and allow the clothes to speak for themselves, rather than embellish excessively.

Le Smoking is also absolutely wonderful; the suit is just perfection. The cut of the jacket and those beautiful trousers – it looks incredibly elegant. It would be impossible to wear it and not look fabulous. When I was younger, I used to take photos of that suit and then cut out the image with a craft knife because it is just the most perfect shape. That suit is sexiness personified.

The house of Givenchy also went through a period when it produced the most amazing coats, which were cut to perfection. Again, for

Patrick Grant
E. Tautz

"Couture is right up there. The touch of a human hand that has imparted time and love and know-how into each garment gives genuine value"

me, it was all about silhouettes. Most of what inspires me in clothing is the cut and the shape: coats with beautiful waistlines; long, full skirts; and enormous collars. They create stunning tailored pieces – that's what I most enjoy. Paul Poiret was also iconic, not so much for the highly embellished pieces but for the later stuff. Slightly ironically, just before he went under, he started creating these really beautiful, simple bi-colour-blocked pieces with no construction at all, which just draped beautifully. There were all-in-ones and two-pieces that were so amazingly coloured – colours that you wouldn't expect to work.

Because I work around beautifully structured tailoring every day, there is no real mystery left for me in construction. I know it's just hard work, years of training, a good hand and a good eye. It might seem magical to people working outside of Savile Row, but not to me – it's what we do every day. Embellishment, for me, is the most magical – the extraordinary way that the ateliers embellish incredibly fine fabrics. Seeing pieces that have been worked into clothes that, if you so much as breathe on them, they would fall to pieces. And the craftsmen have managed to create wonderful patterns on top of them. I know how difficult that is to do. A lot of that work is done outside of the houses anyway. They work for a number of different houses. Lagerfeld, with his Chanel hat on, does it very well. It's so easy for embellishment to look like an afterthought – but Karl's designs look as though it was part of the idea from the very beginning.

I went to boarding school when I was 13, and the wall of my bedroom at school was always covered with images from *Vogue*. In those days there were no British men's magazines, although *Vogue* used to do a quarterly section called "Men in Vogue". I used to tear out the pages and go down to Oxfam or the other second-hand shops and find bits and recreate various outfits. I would often recreate entire looks out of second-hand stuff. It was the complete look that I was trying to recreate. I was less interested in the cut back then.

I don't think there has ever been a time when real luxury has been out of fashion, or not in demand. What we have had for the past 15 years is a bastardisation of the term. And now you have supposed "luxury" brands that are available on the shopping streets of 200 cities across the world, and you can go to any airport and there they all are. That, to me, is not luxury. The whole point of luxury is scarcity, and there's nothing scarce about a handbag that's churned out of a factory and made in the hundreds of thousands. Maybe the people who regard it as special think so because it's very expensive, and to get it they have to go into a shiny shop that's slightly scary.

The men who come to me expect to get a suit

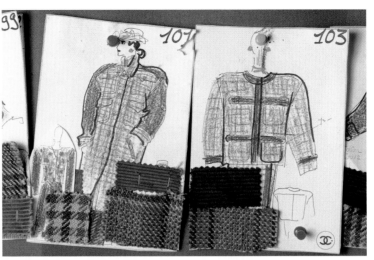

Top, far left: A balloon-sleeved coat in navy wool with wrist-ruffle cuffs, worn with a Garbo cloche hat and a satchel bag, from Hubert de Givenchy's Autumn/Winter 1952 collection

Top, near left: Fashion illustrations complete with fabric samples by Karl Lagerfeld, which are displayed in Chanel's headquarters in Paris

Bottom left: Yves Saint Laurent photographed in 1958 with his models and mannequins in the Dior atelier for the launch of the legendary Trapeze collection. It was his first year as haute couture designer for Christian Dior – the year following Dior's death

Opposite: From Patrick Grant's 2010 menswear collections for E. Tautz, featuring traditional materials such as Harris Tweed, yarn from Jamieson's of Shetland and William Lockie cashmere. The collections, with their focus on classic Savile Row cutting with a touch of signature Grant wit, feature slim-fitting single- and double-breasted jackets and slim, high-waisted trousers, often in bold checks and tweeds

that's unique. Their wives very often go to the couture houses, and every piece that's made for them is unique. There's a time penalty that you have to pay for made-to-measure clothing – it's not immediately available. But the process of having something made for you, and the anticipation you get each time you have a fitting, while that garment is being crafted for you, makes it more valuable. You can't just pick it up off the shelf – just like with certain cars or planes or boats – you have to wait for it. That's what luxury is about, and that kind of customer will never go away.

Couture is right up there. The touch of a human hand that has imparted time and love and know-how into each garment gives genuine value. Couture should be about permanence of beauty and elegance. It would be sad if a couture piece could only be worn for a specific occasion or period of time. It's disrespectful and dishonourable to those people who have put in all those hours if the garment ends up in a cupboard. Couture should be wearable; it's the people wearing it that make it come alive. Without the woman, it's just a rather pointless exercise in artistic expression. Couture should be worn again and again and again.

Biographical Notes

Edward Tautz founded sporting and military tailors E. Tautz in 1867 on Oxford Street. In 1895, Winston Churchill placed his first order there. He went on to become a regular client, as did Edward VII, Cary Grant and David Niven. Tautz was renowned for his sharp cuts and unconventional, innovative fabrics.

Patrick Grant was born in Edinburgh in 1972. He studied at the University of Leeds before taking an MBA at New College, Oxford. His thesis was on luxury British heritage brands.

In 2005, Grant bought and resurrected Norton & Sons, a bespoke tailoring house on Savile Row that was originally founded in 1821 (and which owns E. Tautz). Although he initially ruffled feathers in conservative Savile Row circles, Grant is credited with breathing new life into traditional British tailoring, as Norton & Sons collaborated with young designers including Kim Jones, Richard Nicoll, Henry Holland and Christopher Kane. Grant resurrected the E. Tautz name as a ready-to-wear collection in February 2009 and added a sense of wit. He updated the label's sporting and military heritage with bold colour and pattern, while maintaining the sophisticated Savile Row cut. Grant was the first Savile Row designer to take part in London Fashion Week.

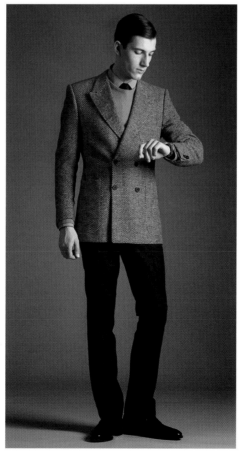

The House of Balmain

The quiet man of couture, Pierre Balmain, shunned the limelight and refused to turn fashion into a spectacle. His determination to remain true to his craft is demonstrated through the purity of his designs and the integrity of his signature style. The only spotlight he embraced was that of the actresses for whom he designed costumes throughout his career. It was here that he played out his whimsical imagination, leaving his couture creations to deliver his vision of understated, superbly refined elegance for which he will always be remembered.

1914: Pierre Balmain is born in Savoie, close to the French Alps. His family owns a wholesale drapery business.

1933: To appease his mother, Balmain studies architecture in Paris, but his heart is in the fashion of the day, which was then in the hands of Chanel, Schiaparelli, Patou, Vionnet, Alix, Lanvin, Molyneux, Lelong and Piguet.

1934: Balmain strikes a deal with his mother that he will try to find employment in fashion and then give up his architectural studies at the École des Beaux-Arts. He tries Piguet, Lanvin and Lelong before he eventually joins Molyneux on a part-time contract. When Molyneux offers him a full-time contract, Balmain's mother is won over. Balmain begins to learn the true art of couture.

1936: Balmain is called to do military service. After a brief spell in Bron, near Lyon, he is called back to Paris, where he continues to work for Molyneux.

1939: Balmain moves to Lelong, another couture house, but Lelong's aesthetic has a more androgynous feel less suited to Balmain's personal style. When Balmain's mother opens a shop in Aix-les-Bains, he returns home. In the summer, war breaks out and Balmain is made secretary to a colonel. Rapidly demobilised, he returns to his mother's boutique.

1941: Balmain is invited back by Lelong and finds himself working alongside a new recruit, Christian Dior, a man who shared his vision for simple yet refined elegance. Together they plan to set up a new couture house under their joint directorship.

1945: Balmain hands in his notice at Lelong and rents a premises at 44 rue François 1er. Balmain's mother sells up and invests heavily in the new venture. On Friday 12th October, the Balmain label is born. After a slow start, and hindered by the aftershock of the war, the debut collection features bell skirts and tiny waists. Alice B. Toklas, Gertrude Stein's partner, dubs it "the new French style". Clients include the Windsors and the Kents. Balmain is also invited to create costumes for the theatre and film.

> "For want of being one who revolutionised, as did Schiaparelli, Courrèges or Dior, I will remain the one who had the courage to refuse"
> **Pierre Balmain**

Creative Director Erik Mortensen, 1987

Pierre Balmain adjusts a model's dress, 1945

Balmain with models in London, 1951

1947: Vent Vert, Balmain's first successful fragrance, is released. A "green" scent, it is created by Germaine Cellier, one of the first female master perfumers. Balmain's rival, Christian Dior, launches the New Look.

1950: Balmain's signature pieces start to appear. He makes shift dresses popular and fur stoles acceptable for day.

1951: Balmain expands. The label opens its first store in America. It proves to be a successful move, with the house showing there one year later.

1952: On 31st July, the Autumn/Winter collection is launched. In the presence of American *Harper's Bazaar* editor Carmel Snow and other leading press, the Jolie Madame collection defines the Balmain aesthetic as it had become and would remain. With emphasised hips and waist, high collars, narrow skirts and rounded shoulders, Balmain had perfected his particular version of elegance, which may have changed in shape over the years, but always maintained its sophistication.

1953: Actresses make regular hops over the channel or the Atlantic to order Balmain's eye-catching gowns. He becomes known as the couturier to movie stars.

1955: A young Karl Lagerfeld joins the Balmain team. He stays for four years.

1960: Balmain is commissioned by Her Majesty Queen Sirikit of Thailand to design her wardrobe for a visit to America.

1961: Vivien Leigh chooses Balmain to create her costumes for *The Roman Spring of Mrs Stone*. In all, Balmain's designs are used in over 30 films between 1947 and 1971.

1964: Balmain releases his autobiography, *My Years and Seasons*.

1968: Balmain designs the "Singapore Girl" uniforms for Singapore Airlines, using the traditional sarong shape.

1982: Balmain dies. Erik Mortensen, his longtime assistant, becomes the label's Creative Director and wins the Dé d'Or award twice, in 1983 and 1987.

1990: Mortensen leaves and Hervé Pierre becomes the Creative Director.

1992-1993: After Pierre leaves the label, Oscar de la Renta is brought on board. He returns to Balmain's '50s-style Jolie Madame look.

1995: French businessman Alain Hivelin invests in the brand. He buys a majority stake in 2005.

2002: Laurent Mercier is brought in to design the ready-to-wear collection. He becomes couture designer in 2002, when de la Renta departs.

2005: Christophe Decarnin, who had designed for Paco Rabanne for 10 years, is announced as Creative Director of ready-to-wear.

2006: Decarnin presents his first collection for the brand. Taking Balmain in an entirely new direction, Decarnin quickly establishes a rock-chic look.

2008: A men's line is introduced.

2009: Sales are predicted at around the $28m mark.

2009: Balmainia hits, with the likes of Rihanna, Julia Restoin Roitfeld and Kate Moss wearing the label.

2010: Decarnin presents a new take on rock culture, with '70s-style fur coats and brocade as key elements.

> "Fashion should reflect the advancement of time and the rhythm of life"
> **Pierre Balmain**

Christophe Decarnin on the runway in 2010

Oscar de la Renta at Balmain, 1993

Laurent Mercier's haute couture show, 2003

WE DIDN'T HAVE A TV until I was about 10. So, from nowhere, I was suddenly thrown into a fascinating new world of frills and jewellery, costumes and feathers, in old black-and-white movies. Whenever I was allowed anywhere near the TV, I became mesmerised. In fact, in my dreams, I was in those movies – waltzing around ballrooms dressed in the most ridiculously glamorous clothing. I think that's where the element of fantasy and playfulness, and not taking myself too seriously, comes from in my own designs. Couture is where you can live like that all the time, because it doesn't have to be realistic. You can live in a dream and pretend you're in a fantasy.

I watched Greta Garbo in *Mata Hari* quite early on and I was knocked out – not just by the costumes but, obviously, by her. The ornate gold dresses and her powerful looks. Movies like that have had a real influence on me – it's surprising how much. It was around that time that I started making stuff for myself, sneaking off to jumble sales and finding myself little high-heeled shoes that my mum would always find and throw away so I would have to get myself another pair. And I would dress up in my mother's clothes and cut her stuff up – I believe that was the beginning of my fashion career.

Lanvin and Poiret right from the beginning were artists. They did paintings, they did fabrics, and they did the most incredible interiors. Everything around them was hand-painted; all the walls were so beautiful. They applied pattern and colour and texture. It wasn't just clothing – they went on to treat fashion as art. They started the celebration of couture as an art form. And they were very different to those who came after them – couturiers who were probably more purists, who focused more on silhouette.

There are now many more constraints on couture. You have to be able to sell it. Not many fashion houses have the luxury of being able to make couture for couture's sake, so now they have to appeal to the people who can afford it. You have to appeal to the Russians or the Chinese; there are only a few Europeans left who can afford it. I think the whole of the fashion industry is changing, because designers have to think so much more about the consumer and their customer.

I hope that one day we can slow down a little bit and celebrate haute couture once more as an art form. Things have become so fast – there's so much to look at. There are extra "pre-collections" in the schedule, and Resort. And yet, there is so little focus on couture. Couture Week seems to happen without us seeing enough of it. But people realise that the fast-fad nation we live in is unrealistic, and they're beginning to

Alice Temperley
Temperley London

"Coco Chanel was inspirational, not just as a female entrepreneur, but also for completely changing the fashion around her"

appreciate quality and originality. People are choosing to spend their money on something that will last and that can be passed down rather than cast aside.

Everything that goes with couture is magical. You have no limit on the fabrics you use. You've got amazing embroidery from Lesage; you've got the facility to be able to create things there and then on the stand; and you're making it to fit someone's body perfectly. My favourite thing in the world is getting on the stand and making garments; creating things in this way is very pure. Then you have to take them apart and make sure that you can put them through to production, that they're practical on a commercial level. But it's that first bit of creativity that's amazing. Couturiers only have to make one of something; they don't have to think about being practical. That's lovely – only making one of something. That's why I love creating wedding dresses so much.

If I could work for any couturier, I would have to choose Balenciaga. He created such an incredible silhouette. He had incredible focus; he was a pure perfectionist. He was a master of cut. He made all his own toiles. It was just him and his craft. And I would love to just sit and watch him at work.

Yves Saint Laurent is interesting, too. He was an extravagant designer. He was one of the first designers to realise that you could have haute couture, but you could apply some essences of the clothes to ready-to-wear. He took elements from the street and elements from couture and mixed them together to make ready-to-wear. I believe he was the first person to do that. We've got him to thank for making fashion more accessible.

Coco Chanel was one of the first designers to bring masculine-inspired clothing into womenswear, and she was obviously a leader. She was also one of the first women to have a successful international business like that. She started out with hats and learned her way from there. She was inspirational, not just as a female entrepreneur, but also for completely changing the fashion around her. Chanel championed the wearing of the trouser and the trouser suit. She had the confidence to turn women's fashion on its head. She came from a very different background, so the fact that she did what she did was also very aspirational.

Is couture fashion in its purest form? Yes, it is pure. But I don't know whether fashion in its purest form comes from the street or from couture. Couture is a different sort of fashion. It's a craft in the purest form. Whereas fashion – I would relate that more to the street. Couture is about fantasy. It's a celebration of a craft. It's an art

Above: Greta Garbo wearing an ornate headpiece made by Adrian Gilbert for MGM's 1931 film 'Mata Hari'

Left: Paul Poiret fitting one of his evening gowns, ca 1930. Poiret, the self-styled "King of Fashion", drew more on his skills of drapery than on tailoring

Far left & above left: One of the Jazz Age's most influential designers, Jeanne Lanvin, approached haute couture as high art, with a focus on intricate trimmings, vibrant colours and virtuoso embroideries. Her designs epitomise the hedonistic age of the flapper

Opposite, from left: Temperley London's Neve and Freesia dresses in monochrome prints from the Autumn/Winter 2010 collection were inspired by the work of fashion photographer Norman Parkinson

form. It's about colour and dreams. It's not really fashion. It's grandeur and splendour.

As a child, I dreamed a lot. I thought that when I grew up I would be like one of the women in the black-and-white movies, and that I would dance around ballrooms in enormous dresses all day long. I thought that was what it was like to be an adult – true indulgence. I guess wearing couture is as close as it gets.

"Couture is about fantasy. It's a celebration of a craft. It's an art form. It's about colour and dreams. It's not really fashion. It's grandeur and splendour"

Biographical Notes

Alice Temperley was born in 1975 in Somerset, and was one of four children. She used to make clothes for her siblings, and make and sell earrings for £1 at the family farm's ciderhouse. She graduated from Central Saint Martins and the Royal College of Art before setting up her own company, Temperley London, in 2000 with Lars von Bennigsen, her then-boyfriend (now her husband as well as Temperley London's CEO).

Temperley London is known for combining British spirit with a dynamic rock'n'roll style; celebrity fans include Heidi Klum, Sarah Jessica Parker, Keira Knightley and Halle Berry.

Temperley is well known for her focus on beautiful fabrics and hand finishes, which led to her being called "the designer making the biggest waves in British fashion" by American *Vogue*.

Alice by Temperley was launched in 2010 as a lower-priced line of easy-to-wear separates, casual dresses, knitwear, statement jackets and accessories. Temperley chose a new generation of British it-girls – including Georgia May Jagger and Amber Le Bon – as faces of the brand.

Temperley's first fashion show was held in London in 2003; in 2005 she showed at New York Fashion Week. For her Autumn/Winter 2009 collection, she hosted a two-day presentation via online video rather than holding a traditional catwalk show. Temperley also has a range of accessories and bridalwear.

Thakoon

I GREW UP IN OMAHA, NEBRASKA in the middle of the US. At the time, I knew that I was interested in fashion, but there were no creative outlets for me. There's just no fashion in Nebraska. I felt very isolated. I was in the middle of nowhere. My only saviour was magazines. I used to go to the newsstand just to look at them, and after a while I found myself gravitating towards fashion magazines – it was a way to be somewhere else, to escape the freezing, mundane place where I was growing up. I always got American *Vogue* and British *Vogue*. I still have all the issues with the covers of Christy Turlington and Helena Christensen. And the one of all six supermodels. So many beautiful fashion stories came out of British *Vogue*; Patrick Demarchelier was shooting for them a lot at that time. That was when I first became absorbed by fashion.

I remember one time picking up a copy of American *Vogue* – I read *Vogue* religiously – it was a couture story with Shalom Harlow; I just remember the fantasy of it, the unbelievable construction, the workmanship. Everything came together for me at that moment. It was the first time that I had actually thought that there was something really special about couture. I think I was probably about 13.

I studied art all the way from elementary through high school. I was always doing art. But when I graduated school I went to college to do business – mainly because I got a scholarship to go to a business school in Boston. But my heart was always in art, although I guess by then my "art" had transformed into a love of fashion.

I don't know if she is considered a couturier, but the most inspirational designer ever is Elsa Schiaparelli. I have always loved her work for the way that she rethought the fashion at the time. She was a revolutionary. She was completely radical. She was so forward, so modern. The surreal things that she was doing have proved themselves to be timeless. I like people who work outside of their time frame. If there is one garment that I wish I had designed, it's Schiaparelli's monkey fur-trimmed coat. It's so daring.

My favourite couturier now has to be Karl Lagerfeld, hands down. He has been so prolific in his career. And he continues to question fashion and where it should be heading. Every collection he puts out for couture – it's always new. In fact, there is never anything that is not new. He never rehashes ideas. He may re-examine techniques, but the way that he does this is always very modern. Karl Lagerfeld has made Chanel. The signature look that exists today is totally his creation. It is his to own. Coco Chanel was also a revolutionary for her time; the idea of a relaxed silhouette when everyone else was doing a structured silhouette was completely radical.

"This new interest in couture-style design is a reaction against everything that is bland. Fashion always works in extremes; that's its essence"

For me, haute couture is all about construction. I admire the handwork that goes into the detail on any couture garment – the embroidery or lacework. But the ease that couture gives is what interests me most. I would love to be able to afford the luxury of creating couture. But you can only do so much before raising the price astronomically. Customisation is a luxury. I try to find ways of constructing pieces that are easy on the body. When you get into the technicalities of construction, only couture quality can make you move as though you don't have on any clothes at all. When you are creating ready-to-wear – which, compared to couture, is semi-mass-producing – how do you capture the spirit of couture? How do you produce clothes that don't feel as though they are restricting you?

There are still women who crave the old-school feel of clothes. There are lots of women who like the freedom of more slouchy clothing, and there are those who like garments that feel a little more formal. Couture's very precise cutting and shaping allows you to move freely.

This new interest in couture-style design is a reaction against everything bland. Fashion always works in extremes; that's its essence. It doesn't move at the speed of a turtle. One season everything is short, the next everything is long; that's the nature of it. But the current trend in ready-to-wear, for special hand-finishing and detailing that emulates couture, comes from a demand from the customer for more than just, say, a T-shirt or a shift dress. It's the opposite of mainstream. It's a desire for something special.

The designer who has had the most influence on fashion is Cristóbal Balenciaga. He paid so much attention to construction and streamlined shapes. He moved fashion to where it is today. I always liked Balenciaga at his most theatrical. For example, I love the single-seam wedding dress. It is genius. Ultimately, couture has to be right for the person who is going to wear it. It's all about the attitude of that woman. The Egg dress was made for someone who wanted that for her wedding day. She had to be comfortable with it. I don't expect any bride would want to look like that today. Although if I were a bride, I would.

I always design clothes to be worn. Fashion should be fun but wearable even if it is avant-garde. If it's unwearable, then it's a costume. Maybe it's like the Balenciaga wedding dress – unwearable by some but not by all.

I really appreciated the documentary on Valentino, *The Last Emperor*. I don't think that people understand the struggle you go through as a designer. They think it is all joy and fanfare. The film made me want to do fashion more. I see the struggle of other people and it gives me drive.

The world of fashion has changed since

Above: A cream two-piece suit by Balenciaga, consisting of a loose top and long, narrow skirt, photographed by Louise Dahl-Wolfe by the Seine in 1953

Far left: An illustration of a bodiced black coat with fox-fur trim by Schiaparelli, from Vogue, March 1934

Left: A Schiaparelli coat with soft, draping folds and fur trim from 1934 – the year she made the cover of Time magazine

Opposite: From Thakoon's Autumn/ Winter 2010 collection: a mixture of textures, including pompoms, ruffles and a variety of furs, were worked into hooded jackets and draped dresses. It was a departure from the vibrant prints with which he made his name

the '70s and '80s, but the world has changed sociologically, too. You can't really blame that on fashion. To be in fashion design, you have to appreciate that things change all the time, and work within those constraints.

In the future, couture will have to adapt to a younger audience. And there's the dichotomy: young people can't afford the prices of couture, but that's what is holding it back. Couture caters for an older clientele, but there are younger customers who can't afford it but who would appreciate it and kick it forward.

For me, couture is about customisation: the ability to get things that specifically fit your body. Who doesn't want that kind of luxury, of having a garment tailored perfectly for you? That idea should be adopted more for ready-to-wear.

My ideas come from everywhere. It's one big stream. They come from art, fashion, from the street, from culture, from hating a trend. All those ideas stream through a tight little funnel and then…out pops a dress.

"When you get into the technicalities of construction, only couture quality can make you move as though you don't have on any clothes at all"

Biographical Notes

Thakoon Panichgul was born in 1974 in Chang Rai in Thailand and, aged 11, moved with his family to Omaha, Nebraska. He was taught to sew by his mother and grandmother, who were both seamstresses.

After graduating with a business degree from Boston University, Panichgul moved to New York City. He worked as a fashion writer and editor at *Harper's Bazaar* before turning his hand to design and enrolling at Parsons The New School for Design.

His first ready-to-wear collection in September 2004 was an instant hit with the fashion industry as well as celebrities including Tilda Swinton, Demi Moore and Sarah Jessica Parker.

After being mentioned by American *Vogue's* Anna Wintour in 2007, he produced a fashion line for Gap, and became a consultant for Spanish retail chain Mango. He also appeared in R. J. Cutler's 2009 documentary *The September Issue*, where he memorably describes Wintour as "the Madonna of the fashion world".

Michelle Obama wore one of his gowns on the evening that Barack Obama accepted the Democratic nomination for president.

ONCE YOU DISCOVER Charles Worth's designs you cannot help but be amazed and inspired. The elaborate gowns that he designed in the second half of the 19th century are quite simply unbelievable. He himself used the history books to inspire his design – he loved fine art and often reworked the textiles that he had found in portraiture. We derive the greatest inspiration from his most extravagant dresses, designed for weddings or the masquerade balls that were popular at the time.

Worth dressed all the celebrities of his day. He was commissioned to design for the stage by actresses like Sarah Bernhardt and Lillie Langtry. And he dressed royalty from all around the world including Empress Eugénie. At some of the royal court occasions in Paris he was behind every single dress – so he had to make sure that they were all different. Who could have imagined that he would truly inspire couturiers for so many generations to come?

The first half of the 20th century was also an incredible time for couture. While Vionnet was draping her mannequins, Schiaparelli was inventing shocking pink and Charles James was conjuring up the most stunning silk ball gowns.

The history of fashion is hugely inspirational. We particularly love looking back at the stars of haute couture history. If we had to choose just one designer who changed the course of fashion, it would be Cristóbal Balenciaga. He certainly always inspires us. He had an incredible sense of volume and space. He transformed the female silhouette with his use of unique shapes.

Another legendary couturier who we admire is Paul Poiret. We love a good revolutionary, and he in particular totally rebelled against the tight corsets that most designers in the early 1900s were imposing on women. This was even before Chanel. Paul Poiret reportedly had a really gregarious nature. In Paris, back in around 1910, he was at the centre of a captivating mix of creative types, from Man Ray and Jean Cocteau to Peggy Guggenheim and Raoul Dufy.

We also often find ourselves looking at the work of Mariano Fortuny. For the pleated silks, of course, but also for the wide array of colours, the intricate beadwork, the complicated prints and the lush velvets. His spectacular creations capture the Art Nouveau genre in fashion. He also dressed Isadora Duncan and Sarah Bernhardt. And, like Worth and Poiret, he looked to the fine arts for inspiration, from Ottoman textiles to Renaissance art. In a sense, perhaps that is what binds all these couturiers together. They have all considered art when they design, and they have turned their fashion into sensual works of art.

In 1999, Valentino Garavani approached us personally. We were both working at Fendi. But

Maria Grazia Chiuri & Pier Paolo Piccioli
Valentino

"Haute couture is a kind of private luxury; it's intimate, a dream that requires constant attention"

we both jumped at the chance to work with Mr Garavani. He is a legend. If you are passionate about fashion, you have to love Valentino. He asked us to create a line of accessories for the maison. Our very first prototype bag was made in the Valentino couture atelier. We subsequently spent a decade working alongside Mr Garavani. He is the master of couture. We have absorbed all we could from his exquisite taste and attention to detail. It was an amazing opportunity.

Mr Garavani showed us how important it is to have faith in your personal vision and see whatever you do through to its proper conclusion. Haute couture is a kind of private luxury; it's intimate, a dream that requires constant attention. To us, the Maison Valentino embodies the best of haute couture "Made in Italy", in a particularly rich style. You will find the highest standards of excellence. Really the craftsmanship cannot be equalled.

When we first arrived at Valentino, the thing that really got us was the insides of the dresses. You cannot believe how elaborate the interiors are. The construction of haute couture is magical, and most people typically don't even get to see it. For our Autumn/Winter 2009 haute couture collection, we turned many garments inside-out, so that we revealed the intricate corsets and constructions, instead of keeping them hidden.

Working in the couture atelier is a wonderful experience. The Valentino premières are really fantastic, they understand our creative vision. They are open-minded people and every collection is a journey in which they are intimately involved. They are a hugely active part of the collection's mood. Most of them had been working for Mr Garavani before and agreed to stay on to work with us. That was very good for us. The transition went really well. Haute couture and fine craftsmanship are the shared passions of us all, so spending time working together creates a very special atmosphere.

The couturier who has probably had the most influence on fashion overall is Christian Dior, with his revolutionary New Look collection after World War II, in 1947. Dior emerged from the unknown to create an original women's collection that shunned the austere looks of the time and revived femininity. His soft, flowing lines and rounded shoulders, those high waists emphasised with belts, the skirts that hit mid-calf, all really changed the tone of fashion.

The house of Chanel revolutionised the industry. Coco Chanel and Christian Dior were absolute masters of couture. They captured both luxury and elegance in the public's mind and left a strong legacy. People continue to refer to them even decades later. They have undoubtedly

Above: A strapless, floor-sweeping gown from Valentino's Autumn/Winter 1990 collection. It was the designer's first haute couture collection to be previewed in France rather than Italy, at the École des Beaux-Arts on 26th January 1989. Reporting on the event, the French newspaper Le Figaro wrote, "For Italy, this is treason: for the first time its foremost and most famous designer has chosen to show his haute couture collection in Paris. This is an unusual and courageous move"

Right: Models in Charles James ball gowns in French & Company's panelled 18th century room in New York, photographed by Cecil Beaton for Vogue in 1948. Charles James was famous for the complexity, beauty and luxurious fabrics he employed in his gowns, which could use up to 25 metres of fabrics such as satin, velvet and tulle

helped maintain the unique allure of couture. And, of course, Valentino Garavani was a master couturier whose influence remains as strong as ever. We were fortunate to work alongside him. To work in a couture house with its founder, that is a very amazing opportunity. For that couture house to be Valentino – that is even better. We have always loved the major glamour at Valentino, and all the elements of its history. We're Italian – we're Roman – Valentino is to us what Yves Saint Laurent is to the French. It's part of our DNA.

Haute couture should be experimental, hand-crafted, extensively researched and unique. In a sense, it is where trends originate in their purest, most unrestrained form. Also, the couture houses help to keep traditional craftsmanship and tailoring alive. This is why it is so crucial that we continue to refer to it. We must jealously protect it. Fashion is about dreaming, and couture is where all the dreams come true.

We love the idea that couture has to be one-of-a-kind, that it has a sense of uniqueness and excess. We like the feeling that couture is special, not easily reproduced, and inspires emotion in the way that some works of modern art do. It's about desire. Yet it is important that couture remain wearable, and we believe that elegance is attained when women wear clothes that they feel confident in.

An haute couture collection always arises from a dream, from an emotion, from a moment of beauty. And there should be a timeless quality to it, as though it doesn't belong to a specific place or generation. By definition, every piece is one of a kind, made to measure.

Some designers limit couture to the red carpet. We prefer to think that elegance should be accessible to everyone. A couturier who can interpret the dreams and longings of every woman is the one who will be successful in the long term. Inspiration can come from anywhere: the cinema, music, illustrations from a book, photographs, an installation at an art gallery… We believe in drawing inspiration from all these and other things, not using them literally as they are, but transforming them, borrowing ideas from them, making them a part of our personal vision. In essence, we find themes in "contaminations" – these unusual mixes from diverse fields. Haute couture is about experimentation; it's a constant work in progress and always a deeply emotional experience. And if you change the way you look at things, the things you look at change.

Which design are we jealous of? Yves Saint Laurent's 1966 Le Smoking suit. We wish we had thought of that. And can you imagine owning a colour? Mr Garavani already did that, with Valentino Red.

The demand for couture has remained constant

Left: A close friend of Paul Poiret as well as Man Ray, heiress and art collector Peggy Guggenheim, photographed in 1924 by Man Ray wearing one of Poiret's revolutionary Bohemian styles. The turban is a common theme in Poiret's collections, and is worn here with a loose, Persian-inspired silk top with kimono sleeves and a full, floor-length silk velvet skirt that creates a slender silhouette; Poiret was considered an artist in the early 1900s and once said, "Am I a fool when I dream of putting art into my dresses, a fool when I say dressmaking is an art? For I have always loved painters, and felt on an equal footing with them. It seems to me that we practise the same craft"

Opposite: From Maria Grazia Chiuri and Pier Paolo Piccioli's Autumn/Winter 2010 haute couture collection for Valentino, which they called The Dark Side of First Love. The duo built on and reworked traditional Valentino motifs such as bows and rosettes, seen here on little black dresses in silk gazar (top right and far right). Chiuri and Piccioli have been praised for attracting a younger generation of fans – and customers – to the world of haute couture

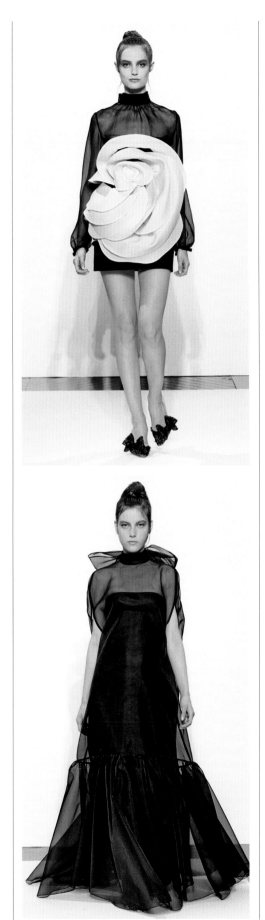

over the years, despite ups and downs in the economy. By couture we don't mean the ostentatious display of designer apparel – an expression of status – we mean the quest for high-quality, special garments and accessories constructed purely for the intimate pleasure they provide. That is what we do.

> "Which design are we jealous of? Yves Saint Laurent's 1966 smoking suit. We wish we had thought of that"

Biographical Notes

The Valentino fashion house was founded in Rome by Valentino Clemente Ludovico Garavani in 1959. Valentino first became interested in fashion whilst in primary school in Lombardy, in northern Italy.

Jacqueline Kennedy famously became a fan of Valentino's designs and ordered six haute couture dresses in black and white to wear during her year of mourning following John F. Kennedy's assassination.

Valentino announced his retirement in 2007, though he continues to be very involved in the fashion house's output.

A feature-length documentary, *Valentino: The Last Emperor,* premiered in 2008 at the Venice International Film Festival.

Maria Grazia Chiuri and Pier Paolo Piccioli have worked together for over 20 years. They trained together at the Instituto Europeo di Design in Rome and met at Fendi, where they worked on some of the house's most iconic bags. In 1999, Garavani personally approached Chiuri and Piccioli, asking them to design a line of accessories for Valentino. Following Garavani's retirement, the duo were appointed Creative Directors of the accessory lines before being made Creative Directors of the house in 2008. They have been credited with infusing the house with a fresh interpretation of glamour. Garavani sat in the front row of their first couture show in 2009.

Jennifer Aniston, Chloë Sevigny, Kate Moss and Sarah Jessica Parker have all worn Chiuri and Piccioli's creations.

MADELEINE VIONNET OFTEN used to take, like, half a year to make one dress. Imagine that. For real couture, that's how long it took.

She invented the bias cut long before anyone had really excelled at this. According to our archives, Madeleine Vionnet first draped her fabrics on the mannequin, then she cut them and hung the pieces for six months or even a year just so she could see how the fabric naturally fell. Once the fabric had "dropped", then she had an understanding of it and could begin the stitching to create the most perfectly draping dress.

The first thing that I do to create the first dress of a collection is to pick up a piece of fabric and begin draping it around the mannequin. It is an instinctive process. It's the beginning of the emotion that you need to create a dress. Sometimes it is stressful, because there is always a pressure to find something new, something different and beautiful.

It's important to start with the fabric. It's difficult to work this way, but it is the most creative. You always need more time. I have always worked like this. I love it. I also love to sketch out ideas, but it's never the same as seeing the effect in a 3D way. You cannot judge the proportion or the silhouette of a dress without actually creating it on the mannequin.

The most inspirational designer? I have to say Vionnet, don't I? How could I say anyone else? I expect many designers would say her. In the past, there have been many amazing couturiers. That period during the '60s was very special, with people like Paco Rabanne and Courrèges. And, of course, Yves Saint Laurent in the '70s. One designer who has helped to maintain the allure of couture is Christian Dior, whose heritage was bound to haute couture since the very beginning. And I have always been fascinated by Balenciaga and the total purity of his creations.

If I could choose one dress to have designed, it would have to be the Paco Rabanne chain-mail dress. I remember seeing a lot of dresses by Versace and Paco Rabanne in chain mail. It still feels very modern.

Over the last year, I've seen a lot of Vionnet's original work. My favourite dress is a very simple black dress – a rectangular pattern – it's so simple and so sophisticated. Her most interesting period was in the '20s – it was a very creative time for her. In the '30s she produced some incredibly innovative silhouettes – this was all ahead of Dior, remember – with huge skirts and transparent fabrics.

My first experience of couture was in Paris when I was a fashion student. I was there to research fashion history. I saw this coat – it

Rodolfo Paglialunga
Vionnet

"The most inspirational designer? I have to say Vionnet, don't I? How could I say anyone else? I expect many designers would say her"

belonged to the mother of a friend. It was a simple but superbly cut Chanel black-and-white houndstooth coat. The lining was bright pink. It was perfect.

Yves Saint Laurent had an ever-contemporary – and at the same time revolutionary – attitude towards fashion throughout his career. I loved his Russian collection – it was very Baroque. An image I always remember is the safari jacket worn by Veruschka. The one where she's holding the gun over her shoulders.

We live in a culture now where we move too quickly. The customers see a dress, buy it and then virtually want to wear it home. Couture has changed completely over the years. In the past, the aristocratic people usually wore only couture. Now just a few women in the world have time to wait for the dress – only a few women can afford it. And clothes have less longevity today – women buy a dress, wear it a couple of times and then put it away in the wardrobe and forget about it.

In days gone by, a woman took a certain pride in looking in her wardrobe and seeing her couture dresses. Couture was valued in a different way. The real frustration is when a customer buys a dress for an occasion and wears it for just one night. For me, the most iconic collector of couture was Tina Chow.

I hope there are still women in the world who truly appreciate those spectacular dresses that are created by the couturiers. Sometimes, perhaps, they design impossible dresses that are too difficult to wear. Christian Lacroix once said that "haute couture should be fun, foolish and almost unwearable", and that is definitely a balanced statement that I agree with, even if my hope is that there is always somebody willing to wear "almost unwearable" clothes. But I think that sometimes people buy these garments because they think of them as art. They don't even buy them to wear.

Karl Lagerfeld once said that "like it or not, everyone has been influenced by Madeleine Vionnet". And so that makes my job difficult. All fashion people love her. I try to do some things differently from her but also to respect her, the brand and the history. It's not always easy. It's a challenge. The designers now at Balenciaga and Lanvin have made something different from the brand. They kept something of the spirit of the original brand but then they did their own thing.

I started just two seasons ago at Vionnet, and I made a deliberate decision to change and to do something in a personal way. Madeleine Vionnet was very scientific. She cut the fabrics in a geometric way. It's so difficult to repeat that. She studied the fabrics for a long time. She would

Left: A floor-length Vionnet one-shoulder dress in a two-tone, bias-cut silk jersey, photographed by Boris Lipnitzki in 1935

Below left: Vionnet at work draping one of her dolls in the '20s, when her reputation and creativity was reaching its height. Her meticulous methods involved cutting, draping and pinning her designs onto the dolls before recreating them on life-size mannequins

Below centre: From 1930, a drawing by fashion illustrator René Bouët-Willaumez of a model wearing a sleeveless gown with a draped bodice and a peplum flounce by Lanvin

Below: An original poster for Vionnet's clothing range from 1919, just a few years after she opened her first salon on the Rue de Rivoli. The poster was exhibited in 2009 at a major Vionnet retrospective at the Musée des Arts Décoratifs in Paris. The house of Vionnet still uses the same logo today

Opposite: Rodolfo Paglialunga's Autumn/ Winter 2010 show for Vionnet included a dress draped from a single piece of velvet, a three-colour silk cocktail dress gathered in the middle (far right) and a fur-trimmed grey dress (right), accessorised with thigh-high boots and chunky bracelets

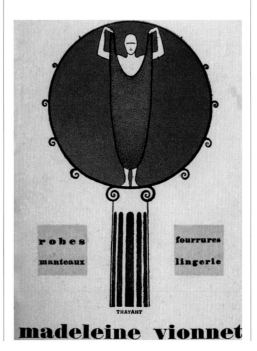

study for weeks and weeks how to make a dress from a single rectangle of fabric. Now we have to work in a very fast way. There is no time to study like she did. But we are used to working fast. Even our private lives move fast. It's not possible to have a lot of time, is it? Probably it's boring to have a lot of time. I don't know – because I never have a lot of time.

An haute-couture piece goes beyond the trends, and its uniqueness is timeless. I would love the luxury of time to design in the old-fashioned couture way, but would I hang my fabrics for six months if I had the option? No, I don't think so. After two dresses, I would feel very old.

> ## "We live in a culture now where we move too quickly. The customers see a dress, buy it and then virtually want to wear it home"

Biographical Notes

Madeleine Vionnet was born in 1876 to a poor family in Chilleurs-aux-Bois, France, and died in Paris in 1975 at the age of 98.

She opened her fashion house in 1912 on the Rue de Rivoli in Paris, and was dubbed "queen of the bias cut" and "the architect among dressmakers". She took inspiration from the modernist dancer Isadora Duncan and the art of ancient Greece.

Her designs were favoured by some of the most famous women of the day, including Marlene Dietrich, Katharine Hepburn and Greta Garbo, and her work dominated haute couture in the '20s and '30s. At one point she employed more than 1,200 seamstresses in 21 workshops.

With the onset of World War II in 1939, the Vionnet house closed. In 1952, Vionnet donated the bulk of her designs and 120 dresses to the Textile Museum in Paris.

The House of Vionnet reopened in 1996 after it was bought by the Lummen family of Belgium. When former Valentino CEO Matteo Marzotto acquired Vionnet in 2009, he appointed Rodolfo Paglialunga as Creative Director, and moved the business from Paris to Milan.

Paglialunga studied at the Marangoni Institute in Milan, and worked with Romeo Gigli for four years before spending 13 years as a womenswear designer working under Miuccia Prada.

Carey Mulligan and Hilary Swank have worn Paglialunga's designs on the red carpet; Jessica Biel, Cameron Diaz and Maggie Gyllenhaal are also fans.

The House of Givenchy

Hubert de Givenchy's association with Audrey Hepburn gives him a Hollywood sheen that belies his mastery. For behind the perfect little suits, flirty dresses, gamine separates and LBDs from *Breakfast at Tiffany's* and *Funny Face*, there stood a serious designer with a purity of line that outshone many of his contemporaries. When he launched the label in 1952, aged just 24, many considered his interchangeable approach to evening separates to be too avant-garde. His later work was thought to share an aesthetic with the master of cutting, Balenciaga. Givenchy brought an elegance and sophistication to the '50s and '60s that cannot be underestimated.

1927: Count Hubert de Givenchy is born in Beauvais, in northern France, the son of an aristocratic family.

1945: After briefly studying law and attending Paris' École des Beaux-Arts, Givenchy gains a position at Jacques Fath.

1947: After brief stints at Piguet and Lelong (where he worked alongside Balmain and Dior), Givenchy moves to Schiaparelli to design separates.

1951: Givenchy opens his own couture house. Due to lack of extensive financing, the first collection is largely made of shirting fabric. The Bettina blouse, named after model Bettina Graziani, is made from a type of cotton usually used only for fittings. The wide neck, fitted waist and dramatic *broderie anglaise* sleeves capture the public imagination, and the blouse becomes a hit. His couture house is across the street from Balenciaga.

> "I've always wanted to create something that would not disappear with me, but would outlive me for 50 or maybe 100 years"
> **Hubert de Givenchy**

1953: Givenchy develops a signature style that is modern yet ladylike. His refined suits, now considered classics, were a radical departure from the prevailing trends of the day. His approach to eveningwear – he created elegant separates that could be mixed and matched – was considered rather too relaxed and informal for the more conservative clients. Younger clients, however, cannot get enough of the new couturier. Givenchy's designs appear on the cover of *Life* magazine. He also begins his associations with Audrey Hepburn and Jackie Kennedy.

1954: The movie *Sabrina* shows Hepburn wearing a wardrobe of Givenchy classics, many with the bateau neckline, which is widely copied. Through worldwide distribution of the film, the designer becomes a household name. He would later go on to also create costumes for *Funny Face* and *Charade*. Givenchy also becomes the first major couturier to produce a ready-to-wear line.

1956: Givenchy establishes a supremely elegant signature that does away with excess decoration. At the same time, he bans the press from his shows, saying, "A fashion house is a laboratory which must conserve its mystery."

Givenchy's Bettina blouse, 1952

Audrey Heburn in Givenchy in 'Sabrina', 1954

Givenchy with his prêt-à-porter collection, 1996

1957: Givenchy and Balenciaga are behind the trend for a look based on silhouette rather than embellishment. The Sack dress is shaped like the head of a rounded flower: full at the waist, skimming the hips and tapering to a narrow hem that finishes below the knee. The shape goes on to become signature Givenchy.

As Hepburn becomes the muse and ambassador of Givenchy, she wears his designs both on- and off-screen. In honour of their ongoing relationship, Givenchy creates L'Interdit, and Hepburn becomes the face of the fragrance long before celebrity endorsements were commonplace.

1961: Givenchy designs the wardrobe for Hepburn to wear in *Breakfast at Tiffany's*. His association with the little black dress begins.

1963: Givenchy designs the outfit worn by Jackie Kennedy for the funeral of her husband, President John F. Kennedy.

1972: The Duchess of Windsor wears a Givenchy coat to her husband's funeral.

1982: Givenchy's success is quantified by *Women's Wear Daily*. His personal wealth is estimated at around $4m.

1988: Givenchy sells his label to LVMH, the fashion corporation that also own Louis Vuitton.

1995: Givenchy retires from designing. John Galliano designs a collection for the brand before moving to Dior.

1996: Alexander McQueen is appointed Artistic Director of Givenchy. He provides a more ornate take on the signature look.

2001: Julien Macdonald is named Artistic Director of the label, and stays for four years.

2005: Riccardo Tisci is appointed Artistic Director, bringing a gothic sensibility to the label. His friend, model Mariacarla Boscono, becomes his muse. His Autumn/Winter collection avoids all references to Hepburn and concentrates on long gowns in nude and black, demonstrating the house's skillful couture craftsmanship.

2006: Tisci's somewhat dark contemporary vision revitalises the brand and Givenchy gains a new generation of fans including Courtney Love, Natalia Vodianova and R&B star Ciara.

2009: Hepburn's Givenchy collection fetches £270,000 at auction.

2010: Tisci breaks taboos by including transgender model Lea T in Givenchy's Autumn/Winter campaign. Model Lara Stone wears a Givenchy dress for her marriage to David Walliams.

"I'm writing my code for Givenchy without destroying its history"
Riccardo Tisci

Riccardo Tisci at Givenchy, 2010

Alexander McQueen at Givenchy, 1996

Julien Macdonald's haute couture line, 2003

AZZEDINE ALAÏA IS THE ONLY real couturier left for me, because he does his own stuff. He has been famous for doing beautiful garments for so long. His technique is extraordinary. He is a genius. He is like a Charles James of modern times. He just concentrates on construction. You can see his single-minded direction. Nothing pollutes his principles. The most magical thing in couture, for me, is what goes into making the garment. I consider a dress to be successful if the art of the construction is hidden... the amount of work and research, and painful toil.

Sometimes I look at the draped dresses by Yves Saint Laurent, and they fall like water from the shoulder over the body; but underneath there is a complicated structure to make that possible, which you never see. The woman's body has been redesigned by the construction. And yet the dress looks like the fabric has been just pinned on the shoulder and not much more than that.

I like many couturiers. There are too many important people I could name. I love the fun of Schiaparelli, the silhouettes from Charles James, the very structural, almost architectural shapes from Balenciaga. But the most important one is Yves Saint Laurent because, when I started work in the '80s, he was a god. For me, he will always be a god. He understood completely the desires of a woman, how women had evolved. He was not simply making clothes, he was studying human philosophy.

My favourite Yves Saint Laurent garment is a man's suit worn with a black sheer blouse. It's very sexual and feminine and powerful all at the same time. Not obviously sexy as fashion can be today, not bimbo sexy – it is so subtle. It's all about the body of the woman. Helmut Newton's photograph of the suit makes a real statement about the subtlety of the sexuality. Yves Saint Laurent has passed now, but it was only a short time ago, so he is still at the forefront of my mind. If somebody says to me, "It's very Saint Laurent," then I always take that as the highest compliment.

Chanel was the first couturier to do sportswear for every day. Everything she did was about ease. You wake up in the morning, you put your clothes on and... done. There was no frou-frou, there was nothing that was not pure. Dare I say she was minimalist? Maybe minimalist is the wrong word – she was more of a purist.

Balenciaga is one of my favourites because he treated each garment like a beautiful, classical architectural piece. It was not so easy to wear, because it was very structural, but at the same time it redesigned the body. I like the fact that he was so inspired by portrait painting. His garments gave the wearer an aristocratic attitude. I love that kind of construction. Today, I work with fabrics that are usually very soft;

Bruno Frisoni
Roger Vivier

"I love pink. There is always pink in the collection. Pink is good because it gives a soft colour to the skin. Pink gives you lightness. Did you ever see anyone looking sad who is wearing pink?"

but for myself I like a suit to be strong and structured, so you have to stand up straight. I love that from Balenciaga.

All the fantasy in the world comes from Schiaparelli. It's surreal, dreamy. It's what I like to do myself. I like to create beautiful design, a purity of design. Then I play with it. I don't care to see the body – I just want to express something. Schiaparelli expressed this both in colour and in humour. I love anything pink by Schiaparelli. I love pink. There is always pink in my collection. Black is good because it redesigns you and white is good for the flesh tones. And black and white together is serious and strong. Pink is good because it gives a soft colour to the skin. Pink gives you lightness. Did you ever see anyone looking sad who is wearing pink?

In 1980 I joined Jean-Louis Scherrer, working in the accessories studio. We had three meetings each season to go through all the accessories. There was a great hatmaker who was very famous in the '40s. She was about 80 at the time – a very nice lady. She came in with this basket full of stuff, including some jewellery. I was in charge of putting the earrings on – one set was a pair of plastic yellow snakes with loads of feathers pluming out from the bottom. Jean-Louis didn't like the feathers, and I knew that a lot of time had been spent putting them on. He told me to cut them off. And I said, "I can't do that, it's impossible." He asked me why. And I said, "Because it's so much work." So he took my scissors and... chop. That taught me a very important lesson that I will always remember: nothing is too good. If it is strong, it is strong; if it is not, then you have to cut it. Now I always cut without any problem.

Since then I have worked in many different couture houses – Chanel, Lanvin and Lacroix. When you see the atelier at work, you can see how amazing it is. The most incredible people work there. They are the most valuable asset of couture. However, there are not many couturiers left now, and what they are doing is not exactly couture any more. It's too much a production for magazine fashion shoots, and not for reality. Couture was different in the past, because ready-to-wear did not exist. Now that there are ready-to-wear boutique collections, you can find garments that are incredibly well made – almost couture. You can order special things.

Chanel is still doing remarkably well but, in the end, are they doing anything particularly new? It's beautiful, incredible stuff, but new? The same is true of Christian Dior. Dior is beautiful; I love it. But it's Galliano's craziness and, for me, it's nothing that's really new. It's a production. These are not new trends. You don't need to find a new way to stand because you

want to wear that kind of stuff. There's not a new fabric that makes a big difference.

Luxury has become mainstream in the past decade; the word is overused. You don't know any more what is or isn't luxury. People think that a cellular phone is luxury. In my eyes, there are two kinds of luxury customer. The French/English customer is after some kind of discreet luxury. Maybe you can't even tell that they are wearing couture. The T-shirt is T-shirt-shaped, but made out of the most beautiful cashmere mixed with silk. But you wouldn't know it unless you touched it. The other sort of customer looks first at the price tag and then, because it's expensive, they want it. And then they mix it with a top from Zara. They seem to choose luxury to gain some kind of recognition. This sort of customer is, to my mind, an aberration.

> "Luxury has become mainstream in the past decade; the word is overused. You don't know any more what is or isn't luxury"

Biographical Notes

Roger Vivier was born in Paris in 1907 and began designing for Elsa Schiaparelli in the 1930s. His best-known creation is the stiletto heel. He made the shoes for Queen Elizabeth II's coronation in 1953, and designed shoes for Christian Dior from 1953 to 1963, as well as Catherine Deneuve's iconic *Belle de Jour* Pilgrim shoes. His shoes have been called "the Fabergé of footwear".

Bruno Frisoni was born in France in 1960 to Italian parents; his mother was a couturier. He has worked at Jean-Louis Scherrer, Lanvin and Christian Lacroix, and collaborated with the houses of Trussardi, Givenchy and Yves Saint Laurent Rive Gauche.

He launched his own line in 1999 and was appointed Creative Director of Roger Vivier in 2004. Frisoni's muse is French model and former Chanel spokesperson Inès de la Fressange.

Frisoni designed a handbag that was inspired by France's first lady, Carla Bruni-Sarkozy, who debuted the bag on Bastille Day in 2009.

Frisoni caused a stir in 2009 with the Dovima shoe, made of gilded silk mesh and jewels and embellished with a pair of birds with gold and crystal heads. The birds could also be worn as hair clips. The shoes retailed for £30,000.

Right: Two models wear sculpted dresses by Charles James, known as America's first couturier: a concentrically flaring fuchsia taffeta gown and a lead-coloured faille gown with underskirt of gunmetal satin

Below: A Schiaparelli hat box in shocking pink, her signature colour, which she described as "life-giving, like all the light and the birds and the fish in the world put together, a colour of China and Peru, but not of the West"

Opposite: Inspired by the Roger Vivier archives and iconic designs, Bruno Frisoni's limited-edition Rendez-Vous accessories collection includes brightly hued crocodile skins, natural materials and printed organza

Matthew Williamson

MY FIRST EXPERIENCE OF COUTURE was at 14 or maybe a year older. I made this little box. I was a big fan of Christian Lacroix even back then, and I was doing some work that was inspired by him. The box was like a treasure box. I was actually rather precious about it. I sent it to Christian Lacroix with a letter. I was basically asking him for a job. I got a really sweet letter back from him saying there was no work there at the moment, but he loved the box. That was my first encounter with a couturier. I am still a massive fan of his work. The first time I met him, I reminded him about my box. I guess he must get boxes all the time. I'm sure it was just one of many.

There's an element of whimsy, of escapism, of fantasy that comes with couture. And that's how it should be, because it's an industry that is largely elitist. It's for the very few women who have the luxury of being able to afford it. It needs to be frivolous and tongue-in-cheek whilst remaining incredibly well crafted. It's an art form in its own right.

I'm sure he has been mentioned before, but I would say the most important designer and the house that has had the most influence on the world of couture has to be Christian Dior. He was such an iconic designer in his own lifetime, and clearly led the way in how women dressed at that time. For that reason alone, I think he will long be remembered as playing a key role in the history of fashion, changing the entire style of how women dressed.

After his New Look collection of 1947, Dior became the most influential designer in the world. And even after the New Look, in the '50s, his sensibility of pared-back minimalism and his clean-line aesthetic carried fashion forward and is still relevant.

The work that Galliano does for the house of Dior now is the modern-day equivalent of what Dior was doing back then. He continues to inspire in exactly the same way the world over. He's avant-garde. He pushes boundaries. He is a true visionary. He has little regard for the zeitgeist – or, rather, he has a single-mindedness when he works – and therefore a unique sensibility. Love it or hate it, I think it is that amount of vision that inspires me. He sticks to his guns. He knows his world and he excels in it. He believes in his vision, and you can feel that when you look at his clothes.

I don't really look at individual garments and wish I had designed them, but there are iconic things in the history of fashion that have gone down as real shifts in how people dressed thereafter. Vivienne Westwood inventing punk, for example. Mary Quant in the '60s. Pucci in Italy inventing speed-dressing in jersey and lycra, and back to Dior as well. My legacy, if I ever have one, would be a more Bohemian way of dressing.

"I find the whole process
of couture magical.
I love this notion
of a blank canvas
and a fantastical vision"

I find the whole process of couture magical. I love this notion of a blank canvas and a fantastical vision, and then all the various processes that go into making any kind of dress or garment.

I have a system in my own business that is almost semi-couture, where we work with clients who want to have a one-to-one relationship with me. It's a great process, because you get to understand the character of the woman, her needs and her desires, which is really at the heart of the couture concept.

I usually do this sort of commission for a special event, a wedding or a party. It's a huge luxury for a designer to be able to work with no strings and no budget requirements. It's a free brief. But anyway, I have always been drawn to the techniques that you find in couture: the craftsmanship, the beading and the embroidery. It's a natural place for me to be, even with my ready-to-wear collection.

There's a continuing trend across the fashion industry for luxury. Right now, for example, there is a demand for a £3,000-plus dress. We accommodate the demand for that in my collections. Then, at the other end of the scale, there are stores that want me to create a dress that a few years ago would have been £700, and they now want that same dress for £400. We are living in a time of extremes. And both of those dresses are necessary and required in every collection.

Obviously, working on the expensive dresses is not only more creative, it's also more rewarding, so I tend to be a fan of those kinds of pieces. Ultimately, though, right now, people are buying cautiously whatever their budget, so a designer's response to that needs to be to offer a product that is really on brand, that is truly representative of the house, and also perhaps consider a more timeless aspect within those pieces. I think there needs to be an enduring sense of quality and craftsmanship. Customers are not buying on a wing and a prayer – they are buying something to keep for years to come.

If I walked into a restaurant and one woman was wearing couture, I wouldn't immediately go, "Oh, she's wearing couture." But if you did a row of 10 women and one was in couture, I'd like to think I would be able to tell, especially if it were suiting – the difference would be obvious because of the techniques involved in making a couture suit. It has been made to measure, so every part of the body has been mapped out and considered. There would be no wrinkle in the fabric anywhere, no bulging at the seams; everything would fit perfectly because everything would be handmade. I think I have a keen enough eye to spot it.

Left: A dress from Christian Lacroix's Autumn/Winter 1987 collection. Williamson was a teenage fan of Lacroix's fantasy creations and followed him as creative head of Pucci in 2005

Opposite: Looks from Matthew Williamson's Autumn/Winter 2010 collection at London Fashion Week. The collection featured asymmetrical silk cocktail dresses and embellished full-length evening gowns with pops of Williamson's signature jewel colours

I'm not sure the concept of couture has really changed over the years. The processes have remained the same. The world of couture remains vital for those designers that still do it. I think it is such a niche industry and therefore it is difficult for the layman to understand it. It is a form of art that only penetrates the top tier of women who buy clothes around the world. You need to have a certain amount of income just to maintain the dresses.

On a personal level, I have always been most inspired by Christian Lacroix. He has an unparalleled sense of extravagance. He has an unabashed love of colour and pattern, and a unique ability to juxtapose fabrics and textures. He uses materials in the most decadent way. This juxtaposition of fabrics has become a genuine passion of mine. Of all the couturiers, I could have learned the most from Lacroix. There is some kind of relationship between what he does and what I do. So that is where I would have felt most comfortable. I'm sure he could have taught me a thing or two. I could have realised my childhood dream.

Biographical Notes

Matthew Williamson was born in Manchester in 1971. After graduating from Central Saint Martins, he freelanced for Marni before working for Monsoon Accessorize.

He launched his eponymous label at London Fashion Week in 1997. The debut collection, called Electric Angels, was modelled by Kate Moss, Jade Jagger and Helena Christensen. His award-winning flagship store was opened in Mayfair, London, in 2004, the year he won *Elle*'s Designer of the Year award.

From 2005 to 2008, Williamson was Creative Director of Pucci whilst continuing at the helm of his own company and launching his own perfume range. He was also given the Moët and Chandon Fashion Tribute Award.

Celebrities such as Björk, Cat Deeley, Sienna Miller, Kelis and Jade Jagger are close friends and fans of his work, and his clothes featured in several of Prince's videos. Prince also performed on the catwalk at the 10th anniversary show of Williamson's label at London Fashion Week in 2007. At the same time, a retrospective exhibition of his work opened at the Design Museum. Two years later, he was invited by the British Fashion Council to return to celebrate London Fashion Week's 25th anniversary.

WHO WAS THE MOST influential couturier in history? I can't say Worth, can I? I can! Charles Frederick Worth was behind so many firsts – in some ways he invented the entire fashion system. He was the first designer to do formal presentations – the forerunner of the modern catwalk show. Also he was the first to put his name on a label in his designs. Separating the year into the fashions seasons – Spring/Summer and Autumn/Winter – that was his idea, too. And his was the first brand to produce a perfume, Je Reviens. He was incredibly creative, had amazing taste and was so full of meaning and fire.

When I look through the archives, everything he created was so sophisticated. He was one of the first designers to be inspired by paintings, finding influences in historical portraits. Surprisingly, he didn't do anything remotely connected to what his contemporaries were doing – no girly pink, for example, or basic colours. The details and shapes were amazing, and this is what I'm trying to create with my work at the brand.

He dressed everybody – from the French Empress Eugénie and the Countess di Castiglione to ladies-in-waiting. He had to ensure that they all had something different but felt good – and that they had a special service. Imagine what it was like walking into a room with all those women wearing massive tulle crinolines and 10-foot lace trains, with incredible jewellery and hair.

I studied at fashion school in Paris, and the classes in fashion history began with Charles Frederick Worth. I remember seeing the label and hearing about the fragrance he developed – Je Reviens – which we're relaunching this year. I was around 19 at the time.

I was first contacted about designing for the new House of Worth in 2003 – for underwear. I didn't immediately say yes, as I had some questions, such as, why relaunch the label now, and with underwear? But then I thought, the brand is so wonderful, something interesting is bound to happen, and I can do something really beautiful. To me it immediately said quality. There is a level of expectation attached to the Charles Worth name. That's very important to me. There aren't many jobs I'd want to do. In fashion you have to choose carefully; you can't jump from one job to the next.

Couture is very important today for the House of Worth. Right now I'm looking at new shapes, for a defining volume for the brand. Couture is not simply about the decorative work – the embroidery or feathers. The work of the *petites mains* is important, but couture is more about discovering the impossible – a shape that can't be done, something that wouldn't be normal for ready-to-wear. It's not for everybody – not just

"I'm not working for a museum. Even if it is couture, even if we just sell a few pieces, there is a woman for each of them"

because it's expensive, but also because there is a precise concept, and it can't fit every woman. My collections are about concept, aura and proportion. Look at my redingote for this season, for example, and you'll see the square shoulders and tiny waist, and how everything works on the inside to make that strong shape.

The construction is everything. The sewing is important, too. First I think about the silhouette, then I put in all the *petites mains* work. Then I choose the fabric, then the colour. I can work separately on all those elements and then put them all together.

I grew up in a family of tailors – men's tailors. This history of tailoring is something that I'm particularly conscious of. I think it's in my DNA – I have a sensibility for cutting and understanding a good line. So menswear comes naturally to me and, some day, I'd love to do it again. But I love a challenge, and I had never done lingerie before.

When I was 20, I worked for Karl Lagerfeld for his own collection for three seasons. I wish I could have stayed longer. It was my first experience of fashion and I was so shy and young. But he was *the one* I wanted to work for. Even now I would go back for a week if I could.

I really appreciate Lagerfeld's work. He has everything: intelligence, talent, and he knows what luxury is. No, it's more than that – he knows how important the people are who do the cutting and sewing. He knows his job well, and how to communicate. He plays the system. He knows how to come out every season with a new concept and silhouette that's different, but not radically so. He understands image, for all the brands he works for, and how to flirt with his customers!

Couture gives you a way to express the best in fashion. There are no restrictions. Ready-to-wear can be very strong, too, but you cannot refine it so much. For my ready-to-wear, I'm taking ideas from couture and making it in a slightly easier shape. I enjoy both – one helps the other along. Everything should be wearable. But some couture is unwearable for certain body types.

I love to see my stuff on a real body or it doesn't make sense; I'm not working for a museum. Even if it is couture, even if we just sell a few pieces, there is a woman for each of them.

There are so few people doing couture now, I feel its techniques are going to get lost. I'm trying to work with as many as I can to keep them in work. I refuse to make anything cheaply. I will not mass-produce in less developed countries for the sake of keeping costs down. Even for ready-to-wear, when you have a budget, I say to my local people, "We have this much money; let's try to make something magical

Left: A princess-style
dress with a flounced
train, in black silk
velvet embroidered
with white lilies and
finished with pearls.
The front bodice and
apron-style skirt are
matched by a deep
shoulder frill in white
satin. The dress is in
the collection of the
Musée de la Mode de
la Ville de Paris

Above: An 1860
portrait by Franz
Xaver Winterhalter
of Eugénie de Montijo,
the last Empress
of France and wife of
Napoleon III, in one

of Charles Worth's
Second Empire gowns
that were inspired in
part by 18th-century
portraiture

Opposite: Four of the
seven designs that
made up Bedin's
Autumn/Winter 2010
collection for the
House of Worth.
The dresses reflect
the founder's much-
loved complicated
constructions,
as well as the
use of extravagant
fabrics and materials
like gold guipure
lace and heavily
detailed embroidery

with that." We have to keep these skills alive.

There is a legitimacy for the House of Worth to be back, because it has a heritage, and we have a responsibility to the past. The inspiration for this collection came from Worth's 19th-century designs, but with a different proportion. I have really just changed the length. What was interesting for me was to retain the richness of Worth, but make it incredibly modern.

I would have loved to have been a couturier in Charles Worth's time, in the golden age of haute couture. There are so many things in the archives that can inspire. It might be a tiny piece of fabric or embroidery. I just need one tiny picture of a detail and I start to dream. Sometimes the dream happens and I need to get it down really quickly before it disappears.

> # "There is a legitimacy for the House of Worth to be back, because it has a heritage, and we have a responsibility to the past"

Biographical Notes

Charles Frederick Worth was born in Lincolnshire in 1825, and worked as a draper in London before moving to Paris in 1846.

With the financial backing of Otto Bobergh, Worth opened Worth & Bobergh dressmakers in 1858. Following the patronage of the French Empress Eugénie, Worth became hugely successful and fashionable, and is widely regarded as the father of couture, elevating the lowly dressmaker to the level of high art.

Under the control of his sons Jean-Philippe and Gaston – founder of the Chambre Syndicale de la Haute Couture – the House of Worth continued to flourish after his death in 1895, only closing its doors in 1956.

In 2010 the House of Worth brand was revived with Giovanni Bedin as head designer. Bedin was born in Vicenza in 1974; despite his early interest in tailoring, he took an accountancy degree before heading to Paris aged 19, to study at the Chambre Syndicale de la Haute Couture. He worked as an assistant to Karl Lagerfeld, and later Thierry Mugler before setting up his own brand.

He showed his first collection for the House of Worth in January 2010. Ballerina-inspired dresses with antique lace corsets and delicate embroidery nod to the founder's signature style.

Jason Wu

I COME FROM ALL OVER THE PLACE: I was born in Taiwan; I grew up in Canada; I moved to boarding school in America; and I went to France for a year. I've been all over the world since I was five. There's a little bit of everything in what I do, and I think that's what makes my style so American – I have this culturally diverse background.

But, saying all of that, there's a real Parisian flavour in what I do. It was when I was living in France that I decided I wanted to become a fashion designer. I suppose this French influence translates to clothes in terms of glamour.

The part of fashion that I love best is the Paris couture techniques. When you look at something I've made, you always have to take a second look, because there will always be some little details that you have missed. That's what I love doing. I love creating beautiful embroideries. I love considered construction. I love perfection and binding the seams inside the garment in a different colour.

I've always been influenced by Jacques Fath, Charles James, Christian Lacroix and Yves Saint Laurent. These are the designers that I really looked up to when I was growing up. If I had to go for one, I suppose I would choose Christian Lacroix. He is definitely the most inspirational; I love what he stood for and I loved his use of colour. He treated couture like a work of art. When I look at his work, it's like looking at a painting; it's so imaginative and so fantastical.

As for Charles James, I've always loved how romantic it all was in the '30s and '40s. His body of work is breathtaking. Sometimes you look at one of his garments and it looks really simple – and then you discover that it has layers and layers of construction under it. To me, that's the essence of couture. Not only is it amazing to look at from the outside, it's also amazing for its construction. It makes you think to yourself, how did they make this? Couture, for me, is all about that – it's got to make you wonder. That's the allure of couture. I apply this principle to my own collections – garments need to be beautiful both inside and out.

Jacques Fath was one of the first couturiers, and his designs were very dramatic. I was watching some old videos the other day of his shows – they were very old-school. There were these models just sauntering through the couture salon. That was in the '50s, a very special time for couture. After Dior's New Look in 1947, that really was the bloom of couture. There was so much to choose from, and it was such an extravagant time in fashion.

One of my first experiences of haute couture was when I picked up a magazine when I was around 10. We had just moved from Taiwan to Canada, and I was learning English at the time. There was a fashion spread of haute couture with Dior, Lacroix and Jean Paul Gaultier. It was shot in a garden. The models were Naomi Campbell and all the other supermodels, all wearing couture. And I was dying to know who they all were and who they were wearing. It got me infatuated with fashion. I hardly knew what a fashion designer was at that point, but it intrigued me and I wanted to know more.

Chanel is one of the best examples of an haute couture house that's as inspirational today as it has ever been. Karl Lagerfeld has managed to keep the image of couture very modern and relevant. He always captures the imagination. As a young designer looking at his shows, I am always inspired.

There are multiple garments that I wish I'd designed: the Venus gown from 1949 by Christian Dior is one of my favourites – it has all these little sequined feather shapes that overlap on the skirt. I have seen it at the Met, and before that many times in pictures. To me, it is pure fantasy, and that is the essence of what haute couture should be. Every single collection of mine is inspired by this idea of fantasy. Even if I do sportswear, you will find that the lining is in organza or the sleeves are trimmed in lace. Little surprising details create a couture feel.

At some point or other, luxury became mass. Fashion was about big logos or how much something cost. Since then, luxury has become exclusive again. It's more about the quality and timelessness of a piece. That's how I interpret fashion. When I create a collection, I look at each garment and ask myself, will this be relevant in five years' time? I have never believed in trends. True luxury is timeless.

I think quite a few couturiers have influenced where we are with fashion today. Chanel is definitely one of them, and Lacroix is another; they're two very different ends of the fashion spectrum and they have made their mark in very different ways. Lacroix has captured so many people's imaginations. I would have loved to work for him. To be inside his atelier would be amazing. His collections were almost pure theatre – they were out of this world. Fashion needs to be like that.

People ask me sometimes, "Why would you show something that's so theatrical, so not wearable?" And I say that fashion should inspire and capture the imagination. Fashion itself is inspired by many things; a show should be a manifestation of its inspirations. Does it matter if you don't sell every single piece on the catwalk? Not really – the presentation needs to be out of the ordinary. Impracticality is in couture's DNA, and it should be pure fantasy.

> "Does it matter if you don't sell every single piece on the catwalk? Not really – the presentation needs to be out of the ordinary. Impracticality is in couture's DNA, and it should be pure fantasy"

The two historical houses that most maintain the status of couture are Chanel and Dior. They both capture the magic. Couture is much smaller now; far fewer people are doing it in the traditional way. Christian Dior has been kept alive by Galliano. Ready-to-wear used to be a million miles away from couture, but that has changed radically. With modern technology, we are able to be more elaborate. We can laser-cut a fabric now, and do embroidery, and create synthetic materials. Playing with these ideas as a ready-to-wear designer gives a couture feel.

The best fashion themes come from outside of fashion. It's important to look for ideas outside of the industry, but I also can't help but look at couture designers. It's hugely important for fashion designers – especially young fashion designers – to look at the history of fashion, to study the people who paved the way for us and who allow us to do what we do today, to make our own history. It is impossible to create the future without knowing the past.

"After Dior's New Look in 1947, that really was the bloom of couture. There was so much to choose from, and it was such an extravagant time"

Biographical Notes

Jason Wu was born in Taiwan in 1982 and moved to Vancouver at the age of nine; he is now based in Manhattan. He learned to sew by making dolls' clothing, and at the age of 16 had begun designing a line of dolls' clothes for Integrity Toys.

He studied at Parsons The New School for Design and worked as an intern for Narciso Rodriguez in New York.

Wu's first collection was in 2006, and he won the Fashion Group International's Rising Star Award in 2008. Early clients included Ivanka Trump, January Jones and Amber Valletta.

Anna Wintour was in the front row of Wu's show at New York Fashion Week in 2008.

Wu became an international name overnight when Michelle Obama wore his specially designed asymmetrical white chiffon dress to the inaugural ball in 2009.

In June 2010, Wu won the Swarovski Award for Womenswear at the CFDA Fashion Awards.

Above: Surrounded by models wearing his couture collection for Spring/Summer 1954, Jacques Fath adjusts one of his designs

Above centre: A Jacques Fath satin sheath with a fishtail skirt and gold embroidery

Above right: Christian Dior's Venus wedding gown of grey silk tulle overlaid with scallop-shaped petals, photographed by Willy Maywald for Dior's Autumn/Winter 1949-1950 collection. It is now in collection of the Metropolitan Museum of Art in New York

Below right: A broad-striped, voluminous bubble dress from Balenciaga's Autumn/Winter 1958 collection

Opposite: Looks from Jason Wu's Autumn/Winter 2010 collection, inspired by Irving Penn. The polka dots on the shantung bubble dress (bottom right) are in fact printed representations of cigarette burns enlarged from one of Penn's prints. Wu also nodded towards traditional couture craftsmanship, seen here on a floor-length silk tulle gown embroidered with gilded leaves (top left)

Index

Bibliography

Baudot, F., *Alaïa* (Assouline, New York, 1996)
Baudot, F., *Chanel Fine Jewellery* (Assouline, New York, 2003)
De la Haye, A. and Tobin S., *Chanel: The Couturiere At Work* (Victoria & Albert Museum, London, 1994)
De Marly, D., *Worth: Father of Haute Couture* (Elm Tree Books, London, 1980)
Dior, C., *Dior by Dior* (1957; rpt. V&A Publications, London, 2007) Citations refer to the V&A edition
Golbin, P. ed., *Balenciaga Paris* (Thames and Hudson, London, 2006)
Golbin, P., *Valentino: Themes and Variations* (Rizzoli, New York, 2008)
Hambourg, M. M., Heilbrun, F., and Néagu, P., *Nadar* (The Metropolitan Museum of Art, New York, 1995)
Jebb, M. ed., *The Diaries of Cynthia Gladwyn* (Constable, London, 1995)
Jouve, M-A., *Balenciaga* (Thames and Hudson, London, 1997)
Lacroix, C., and Mauriès, P., *Pieces of a Pattern: Lacroix by Lacroix* (Thames and Hudson, New York, 1992)
Mears, P., *Madame Grès: Sphinx of Fashion* (Yale University Press in association with the Fashion Institute of Technology, New York, 2007)
Merceron, D. L., *Lanvin* (Rizzoli, New York, 2007)
O'Hara Callan, G., *Dictionary of Fashion and Fashion Designers* (1986; rpt. Thames and Hudson, London, 1998)
Pochna, M-F., *Dior* (Assouline, New York, 2008)
Poiret, P., *King of Fashion* (1931; rpt. V&A Publications, London, 2009) Citations refer to the V&A edition
Rawsthorn, A., *Yves Saint Laurent* (HarperCollins, London, 1996)
Rubin, J. H., *Nadar 55* (Phaidon Press Limited, London, 2001)
Salvy, G-J., *Balmain* (Editions du Regard, Paris, 1996)
Schatzberg, J., *Paris 1962: Yves Saint Laurent and Christian Dior – The Early Collections*, (Rizzoli, New York 2007)
Schiaparelli, E., *Shocking Life* (1954; rpt. V&A Publications, London, 2007)
Spanier, G., *It Isn't All Mink* (1959; rpt. Cedric Chivers Ltd, Bath, 1971)
Taylor, L., and Wilson, E., *Through the Looking Glass: A History Of Dress From 1860 to the Present Day* (BBC Books, London, 1989)
Wilcox, C. ed., *The Golden Age of Couture* (V&A Publications, London, 2007)

Notes

1. Galliano, Harrods interview, 2010
2. De Marly, p.7
3. Dickens, Charles *All The Year Round*, June-Dec 1867, Vol IX, p.9, quoted in De Marly, p.99
4. Poiret, p.30
5. Dior, p.15
6. Poiret, p.77
7. De La Haye & Tobin, p.59
8. Wilcox, p.14
9. Jouve, p.6
10. Poiret, p.45
11. Jouve, p.6
12. Dior, p.36
13. Dior, p.147
14. Rawsthorn, p.33
15. Vreeland, Diana, ed., *Yves Saint Laurent*, p.7, Metropolitian Museum of Fine Art (New York, 1983) quoted in Rawsthorn, p.43
16. Galliano, Harrods interview, 2010

Picture Credits

All designer portraits by Rankin

Every effort has been made to seek permission to reproduce all images. Any omissions are entirely unintentional, and the details should kindly be addressed to Harrods Publishing.

Unless otherwise stated, all contemporary collection photographs are courtesy of the respective fashion house.

Page 2: Rex Features. 6: Frances McLaughlin-Gill/Condé Nast Archive/Corbis. 8-15: TopFoto (Worth atelier, Worth, Poiret, Balenciaga, Dior, YSL); Roger Viollet/Getty Images (Lanvin, Gres); Roger Viollet/Rex Features (Vionnet); Time Life Pictures/Getty Images (Schiaparelli); Lipnitzki/Roger Viollet (Chanel); Sunset Boulevard/Corbis (Givenchy); Ron Galella/WireImage (Lacroix); Popperfoto/Getty Images (Amies); Frederic Souloy/Gamma, Camera Press London (Lagerfeld). 18-21: Bettmann/Corbis (Chanel); Pierre Mourgue (Rochas). 22-27: Getty Images (Dietrich); Columbia/The Kobal Collection/Bob Coburn (Hayworth); Time & Life Pictures/Getty Images (YSL); Metropolitan Museum of Art/Art Resource/Scala, Firenze (Vionnet); Chris Moore (contemporary collection). 28-31: TopFoto (Givenchy); Henry Clarke/Condé Nast Archive/Corbis (Balenciaga); Dan and Corina Lecca (contemporary collection). 32-33: Bettmann/Corbis (Dior); Willy Rizzo (Trapeze); Roger-Viollet/Rex Features (Bohan); Julio Donoso/Sygma/Corbis (Ferre); Ken Towner/Rex Features ('97 Dior Couture); Anthea Simms (Galliano). 34-37: Henry Clarke, Musée Galliera, ADAGP, Paris and DACS, London 2010 (Balenciaga); TopFoto (Dior); Time & Life Pictures/Getty Images (Chanel). 38-41: Anthea Simms (Lacroix); Association Willy Maywald/ADAGP, Paris and DACS, London 2010 (YSL); Chris Moore (contemporary collection). 42-45: Empire Pictures Inc/Photofest (YSL); Jack Robinson/Condé Nast Archive/Corbis (de la Falaise); Jean-Claude Deutsch/Paris Match/Scoop, Camera Press London (Deneuve). 46-49: Time & Life Pictures/Getty Images (Balenciaga); Clifford Coffin/ Condé Nast Archive/Corbis (Fath); Metropolitan Museum of Art/Art Resource/Scala,

Firenze (Schiaparelli); Peter Ashworth (contemporary collection). 50-51: Bettman/Corbis (Chanel/Smith); Douglas Kirkland/Corbis (Chanel); TopFoto (LBD); AFP/Getty Images (Lagerfeld); Abbas/Magnum Photos (Fressange); Anthea Simms (Lagerfeld). 52-55: Louise Dahl-Wolfe/Staley-Wise Gallery (Balenciaga); Dan Lecca (contemporary collection). 56-61: Metropolitan Museum of Art/Art Resource/Scala, Firenze (Poiret); Christian Berard/Condé Nast Archive/Corbis (Patou); René Gruau (Dior); Topfoto (Schiaparelli); Marcio Madeira/FirstView (contemporary collection). 62-65: Thierry Perez (Alaïa); Getty Images (Grace Kelly); FirstView (Le Smoking). 66-69: G. Hoyningen-Huene/R.J. Horst/Staley-Wise Gallery (Balenciaga); Sipa Press/Rex Features (Mugler); V&A Picture Library (Schiaparelli); Chris Moore (contemporary collection). 70-71: White Images/Scala, Florence (illustration); Edward Steichen/Condé Nast Archive/Corbis (Organdy dress); Harlingue/Roger Viollet/Getty Images (Lanvin/model); Bettmann/Corbis (Castillo-Lanvin); Pierre Vauthey/Corbis Sygma (Crahay); Anthea Simms (Elbaz). 72-75: Horst P. Horst/Vogue/Condé Nast Archive (Vionnet); Sipa Press/Rex Features (Grès); Dan Lecca (contemporary collection). 76-79: Edward Steichen/Condé Nast Archive/Corbis (Vionnet); Getty Images (Chanel). 80-83: Nicolas Fassbind/Rapho/Gamma, Camera Press London (Rabanne); Popperfoto/Getty Images (Cardin); Chris Moore (contemporary collection). 84-87: C.J Tavin/Everett/Rex Features (Seyrig); Astor Pictures/Photofest (Marienbad). 88-89: Time & Life Pictures/Getty Images (Polka Dot); TopFoto (Fabiola); V&A Picture Library (Cape) Henri Cartier-Bresson/Magnum Photos (Balenciaga); Thierry Orban/Corbis Sygma (Thimister); Anthea Simms (Ghesquière). 90-95: UPPA/Photoshot (Chanel); Henry Clarke, Musée Galliera, ADAGP, Paris and DACS, London 2010 (Lanvin-Castillo); John Rawlings/Condé Nast Archive/Corbis (Balenciaga); Pierre Morgue (Balenciaga 1946 illustration); Bernard Blossac (Balenciaga 1957 illustration), Dan Lecca (contemporary collection). 96-99: Association Willy Maywald/ADAGP, Paris and DACS, London 2010 (YSL); Time & Life Pictures/Getty Images (Dior). 100-103: Bettmann/Corbis (Kelly); Getty Images (Givenchy);

Andrea Klarin (Valentino); Frédérique Dumoulin (contemporary collection). 104-105: Bettmann/Corbis (YSL); Sipa Press/Rex Features (Mondrian); Alain Nogues/Sygma/Corbis (Le Smoking); David Thorpe/Rex Features (Safari); Thierry Orban/Sygma/Corbis (YSL couture); WWD/Condé Nast/Corbis (Pilati). 106-111: Getty Images (Vionnet); Condé Nast Archive/Corbis (Pages); Hiro (Balenciaga); V&A Picture Library (Schiaparelli). 112-115: Hulton-Deutsch Collection/Corbis (YSL); Everett Collection/Rex Features (Givenchy). 116-119: Time & Life Pictures/Getty Images (Givenchy); Massimo Listri/Corbis (fashion drawings); Willy Rizzo (YSL). Angelo Pennetta & John Akehurst (contemporary collection). 120-121: Corbis (Balmain); Getty Images (furs); Sipa Press/Rex Features (Mortensen); Bruno Barbey/Magnum Photos (de la Renta); Christopher Moore (Mercier); Anthea Simms (Decarnin). 122-125: Patrimoine Lanvin (illustrations); Popperfoto/Getty Images (Garbo); Underwood & Underwood/Corbis (Poiret). 126-129: Louise Dahl-Wolfe/Staley-Wise Gallery (Balenciaga); White Images/Scala, Firenze (illustration); Roger Viollet/Getty Images (Schiaparelli). 130-135: Donato Sardella/Condé Nast Archive/Corbis (Valentino); Cecil Beaton/Condé Nast Archive/Corbis (James); Collection Rijksmuseum (Peggy Guggenheim); Valentino/SGP Italia (contemporary collection). 136-139: Roger Viollet/Getty Images (Vionnet); Rene Bouet-Willaumez/Condé Nast Archive/Corbis (Lanvin); Getty Images (Vionnet poster). 140-141: Time & Life Pictures/Getty Images (Bettina); Bettmann/Corbis (Hepburn); Corbis (Givenchy; McQueen); Philippe Wojazer/Reuters/ Corbis (Macdonald); Anthea Simms (Tisci). 142-145: Cecil Beaton/Condé Nast Archive/Corbis. 146-149: Pierre Vauthey/Sygma/ Corbis (Lacroix); Dan Lecca (contemporary collection). 150-153: Nadar/The Granger Collection/TopFoto (Comtesse de Greffulhe); Franz Xaver Winterhalter (Eugénie); House of Worth/Piero Biasion (contemporary collection). 154-157: Walter Carone/Parismatch/Scoop, Camera Press London (Fath); Association Willy Maywald ADAGP, Paris and DACS, London 2010 (Dior); Tom Kublin (Balenciaga); Dan Lecca (contemporary collection).

160